TWAYNE'S WORLD AUTHORS SERIES

A Survey of the World's Literature

Sylvia E. Bowman, Indiana University

GENERAL EDITOR

GERMANY

Ulrich Weisstein, Indiana University

EDITOR

Angelus Silesius

(*TWAS 25*)

TWAYNE'S WORLD AUTHORS SERIES (TWAS)

The purpose of TWAS is to survey the major writers —novelists, dramatists, historians, poets, philosophers, and critics—of the nations of the world. Among the national literatures covered are those of Australia, Canada, China, Eastern Europe, France, Germany, Greece, India, Italy, Japan, Latin America, New Zealand, Poland, Russia, Scandinavia, Spain, and the African nations, as well as Hebrew, Yiddish, and Latin Classical literatures. This survey is complemented by Twayne's United States Authors Series and English Authors Series

The intent of each volume in these series is to present a critical-analytical study of the works of the writer; to include biographical and historical material that may be necessary for understanding, appreciation, and critical appraisal of the writer; and to present all material in clear, concise English—but not to vitiate the scholarly content of the work by doing so.

Angelus Silesius

by JEFFREY L. SAMMONS

Yale University

Twayne Publishers, Inc.   ::   New York

Preface

Of the rich and varied literary life in seventeenth-century Germany, only a relatively small part has maintained a place in the living heritage of literature. Grimmelshausen's stupendous novel *Simplicius Simplicissimus*, the agonized poetry of Andreas Gryphius, Paul Gerhardt's Protestant hymns, and a handful of isolated poems—these are virtually the only works of that period that have found extensive appreciation in other times and places. There is more than one reason for this. In order to create a literature at all, the seventeenth century had to wrestle mightily with an undeveloped language and formal theory, and the sweat and struggle is sometimes awkwardly evident in a way that compares unfavorably with contemporary writing in France, England, Italy, and Spain. Furthermore, most of the attitudes and issues of that age are not our own. For centuries the aristocratic bias and function of much of the writing have had little appeal. It is also true, however, that the eighteenth century, at the beginning of a development that was to lead to the most glorious period in the history of German literature, found it necessary to turn sharply against the whole esthetic experience of the recent past and thus managed rather unfairly to barricade the vision of later generations into that period. It is only in more recent times that a renewed appreciation of the so-called Baroque period in German literature has developed.

But there has always been a second line of writers who have captured the attention of literary men and thinkers, if not of the general public, in a tradition almost unbroken for three hundred years. The foremost among these is undoubtedly the religious poet Johann Scheffler, the self-styled Silesian Angel.

A considerable gap seems to separate our age from one in which a poet could in all seriousness give himself such a nom de plume.

The difference in style and bearing is undeniable, but paradoxically enough, it is because there are certain analogies between the circumstances of life in his time and in our own that modern men have turned their attention to the achievements of that period. In Scheffler's time, a large part of Europe was devastated by a great and hideous war. Two impressive and confident ideological systems were fighting for the whole allegiance of men, and these systems were purportedly, but in fact inexactly, aligned with two groups of political powers, so that the spiritual issues became inextricably intertwined and confused with raw imperialist politics. A great deal of luxury, some magnificent, some tawdry, radiating out from one of the great powers, was widely imitated, as though it could somehow neutralize the vast miseries of the time. The souls of many men were adrift; some were permeated by ineradicable anxiety, and others cast tensely about for new solutions and better faiths; at the same time there were slight signs that a new order of human affairs and ideas was developing that would bring a little light and peace into the future. The parallels between that time and this are too obvious to require elaboration. It is in this context that Johann Scheffler, in a brief outburst of genius, compressed one solution to the dilemma of man into some of the most astonishing verses ever written in German.

This study attempts to give an introduction to Scheffler's entire literary career, and begins with an account of his life. In the discussion of his works, the emphasis remains, as it must in any treatment of the subject, upon Scheffler's masterpiece, the *Cherubinic Wanderer,* but attention is given to his two other major poetic works as well. Furthermore, a chapter has been devoted to some considerations upon his later polemical writings, because they are often neglected and sometimes misrepresented in studies of Scheffler, and a concise, reliable view of them is not easily available. The bibliography includes Scheffler's publications (with the exception of individual pamphlets) and the important modern editions and translations of them; no effort has been made to list the numerous editions of selected poems. It would have been pointless for the purposes of this study to give an exhaustive bibliography of the secondary literature, for much that has been written about Scheffler is of indifferent value; the selection offered here contains the most important scholarly studies, those essays that have played a part in the controversy surrounding the theological content of Scheffler's poetry, and a few general presentations. A very thorough bibliography up to the 1940's will be found in Henri Plard's edition and French translation of the *Cherubinic Wanderer, Pèlerin chérubinique* (Paris: Aubier, 1946); standard bibliographical aids satisfactorily supplement that list up to the present.

In my own translations I have made no attempt to do anything but reproduce the sense. A genuinely faithful translation of Scheffler would require the idiom of Vaughn, perhaps, or Crashaw, a language of which I am not master. Furthermore, the effort to produce a rhymed metrical version in English often distorts the sense. In the case of the *Cherubinic Wanderer* I have supplied metrical translations from the collections of Paul Carus, J. E. Crawford Flitch, Julia Bilger, and Willard R. Trask, with appropriate acknowledgment; elsewhere I have given exact prose translations, in the hope that the combination of both would give the flavor of Scheffler's sound as well as the literal meaning where it is important.

JEFFREY L. SAMMONS
New Haven, Connecticut

Acknowledgments

Acknowledgment is due to The Peter Pauper Press for permission to quote the *haiku* on p. 37; to Random House, Inc., for permission to quote the translations of Trask; and to George Allen & Unwin Ltd. for permission to quote the translations of Flitch. Special thanks are due to Mrs. Walter J. Coates of North Montpelier, Vermont, for graciously permitting me to quote the translations of Julia Bilger.

I owe a particular debt of gratitude to three scholars: to Professor Ulrich Weisstein of Indiana University, whose patient editing yielded many valuable suggestions; to the late Curt von Faber du Faur, from whose immense erudition I have greatly profited and whose death in January, 1966, has prevented me from putting this book into his hands as I had hoped to do; and to Professor Christoph Schweitzer of Bryn Mawr, who a number of years ago first conducted me into the world of the *Cherubinic Wanderer*. All responsibility for the facts and judgments in this study is, of course, exclusively my own.

Contents

Chronology

1624   Johann Scheffler born at the end of December in Breslau.

1637   Death of Scheffler's father.

1639   Death of Scheffler's mother.

1639-   Scheffler attends the *Elisabethgymnasium* in Breslau.
1643

1643   Matriculation at the University of Strassburg.

1644   Transfer to the University of Leiden.

1647   Matriculation at the University of Padua.

1648   Ph.D. and M.D.

1649   Appointed court physician to Duke Sylvius Nimrod at Oels.

1652   Scheffler's friend Abraham von Frackenberg dies.
       Scheffler comes into conflict with the Protestant censor.

1653   Conversion to Roman Catholicism; Scheffler takes the name Johann Angelus.

1654   Honorary appointment by Emperor Ferdinand III as Imperial Court Physician.

1657   First editions of the *Cherubinic Wanderer* and the *Holy Joy of the Soul*.

1661   Scheffler ordained a priest.

1663   The *Turkish Pamphlet* opens twelve years of public polemic.

1664-   Court marshal to the Prince-Bishop of Breslau.
1666

1668   Second edition of the *Holy Joy of the Soul* with a fifth book added.

1674   *Sensual Description of the Four Last Things* (imprint 1675).

1675   Second edition of the *Cherubinic Wanderer* with a sixth book added.

1676   *The Precious Evangelical Pearl* (translation).

1677   *Ecclesiologia.* Scheffler dies in Breslau July 9.

CHAPTER 1

Pilgrimage into Isolation

I *Birth into an Anxious Land*

JOHANN SCHEFFLER lived before the age when writers thought of themselves as important and interesting public personalities in their own right. The anonymity of the Middle Ages was, of course, long since a thing of the past, but the letters and memoirs, written and preserved with posterity looking over one's shoulder, belonged to the future. Consequently, for the most part Scheffler's life must be pieced together out of official documents with only occasional, and sometimes not very reliable, personal evidence. Owing to the painstaking labor of scholars, we are able to give a fairly complete account of the external events of his career; but there are shadowy periods, and even worse, the actual rationale of his peculiar personality cannot be ascertained with more than speculative probability.

Scheffler was born at the end of December, 1624, in Breslau. Both the date and the place have significant associations. The year 1624 saw the death of the inspired shoemaker Jakob Böhme (b. 1575), the most recent representative of the German mystical tradition, and of the Spaniard St. John of the Cross (b. 1542), an important figure in the line of neo-Catholic mystics. It was also the year of Martin Opitz's (1597–1639) *Buch von der Deutschen Poeterey* (*Book of German Poetics*), a slender, derivative, and incomplete study which, nevertheless, was to have an electric effect upon the German effort to create the language and sense of form that made Scheffler's poetry possible. When Scheffler was born, the Thirty Years' War was going into its seventh year, and he was to be twenty-three before the chaos was put to an end and the Treaty of Westphalia more or less re-established the *status quo ante*. The war raged with particular violence in Silesia, flowing around Breslau in waves of bloodletting, marauding, and destruction; the figures adduced for the loss of population in the course of the war sometimes strain belief. Although in our own century we have seen horrors that dwarf those of that time, it should be remembered that this part of the world had been at relative peace since the agreement of Schmalkalden in 1555, and the generation that witnessed the war was unused to such experiences on such a large scale. It has often been suggested that the pervasive gloom of the poetry of Andreas Gryphius (1616–64), whose life was by no means particularly unhappy, was conditioned by his youthful experiences of the war in Silesia. That country is also the part of Germany that, from the Middle Ages to relatively recent times, has produced thinkers and writers of a strong mystical bent; Scheffler was, as it were, born to the mystical tradition. Finally, in later years, Silesia was one of the places where the political and ideological struggles accompanying the Counter Reformation were the most exacerbating and difficult. All these elements played their part in the poet's career and vision.

Scheffler's father, Stanislaus, was a Protestant from Poland, born in the neighborhood of Cracow around 1562. Although clearly of German culture, he possessed a patent of minor nobility from the Polish crown as Lord of Borwicze and regarded himself as a Polish citizen. Why he left Poland is not clear; perhaps the position of a Protestant in the Catholic kingdom was not comfortable. In any case, he moved to Breslau no later than 1619. How he earned his livelihood is also unknown; but records of a number of lending transactions show that he was clearly a man of property, and his son inherited a tolerable fortune. On February 20, 1624, the sixty-two-year-old gentleman married a twenty-four-year-old girl named Maria Hennemann, and their son was born before the year was out.

As nearly as we can reconstruct it, the family does not seem to have been a particularly happy one. Stanislaus was not only nearly forty years older than his wife but was apparently of a rather blustering temperament. We have a record of an official reprimand given to him for his manner of pressing a legal claim even though he was judged to be in the right.[1] Furthermore, another of his sons, Johann's younger brother, Christian, was feeble-minded and in later life had to be assigned to guardians. Stanislaus died on September 14, 1637, when Scheffler was only twelve, and his young wife died a year and a half later on May 27, 1639;

[16]

the phrasing of her death notice[2] suggests that her life had been a troubled one. At the age of fourteen, therefore, Scheffler was an orphan. One can only speculate on what effects these childhood experiences may have had on him. But if we imagine that his life with an apparently harsh, difficult, and impulsive father, and a troubled, not very strong mother, both of whom were then lost at an early age, might have led to a habit of turning his attention inward, along with a distinct tendency to emotional dependence, it would not contradict anything we know about this character.

II *A Humanistic Education*

It is not known who took over the care of young Scheffler and his brother and sister. Whatever the arrangement, there is no evidence that it did not work satisfactorily. In any case, his guardians saw to it that he received an excellent humanistic education. From 1639 to 1643 he attended the renowned *Elisabethgymnasium* in Breslau, a school under the direction of a gifted pedagogue named Elias Major. The most important influence on young Scheffler was undoubtedly that of Christoph Köler (1602–58), a rather unsteady character who was, however, one of the followers of Martin Opitz and, indeed, wrote the first biography of Opitz after the latter's death in 1639. There can be no doubt that the gospel of an awakening German literature was preached in this school with enthusiasm. In fact, one of Scheffler's schoolmates, Andreas Scultetus (i.e., Schultz: 1622–47), before his early death wrote some smooth and clear poetry in the spirit of Opitz, which was not much noticed in his own time but subsequently captured the attention of Lessing.[3] Scheffler himself seems not only to have been an outstanding student throughout his school days but seems also to have joined in the literary activities which were part of the program in the *Gymnasium*.

Although it is hard to believe that Scheffler did not write a great deal of poetry during his school and university years, we possess only a handful of examples. Scheffler's youthful poems were all written for special occasions, in the style of the age; they are controlled and competent with strictly maintained meters and pure rhymes (no longer such a great achievement in the 1640's as it had been twenty years before), but they give little indication that a great poet was developing. Except for a Greek encomium upon the rector of the *Gymnasium,* written in 1641,[4] all the preserved poems are in German. From that year we have a competent but undistinguished sonnet on the name day of one of his teachers, Chrisostomus Schultz,[5] and a poem on the death of a certain Johann Blaufuss.[6] The latter is somewhat more ambitious, consisting of eleven stanzas of six four-beat lines each, ryhmed *ababcc.* It is constructed upon the well-worn conventional topos of life as a voyage upon a stormy sea; the Christian is certain of reaching the port of death in a state of calm and blessedness. This argument is applied first to Blaufuss, then expanded in the last three stanzas to a general statement about the situation of man. The poem, though slight, is structurally well controlled. What is interesting about it in the light of Scheffler's later development, however, is the complete lack of any elegiac tone. Even in the seventeenth century it is unusual for an occasional poem on the death of an individual to express no note of grief and to insist exclusively that death is a welcome escape from this vale of tears into the blessedness of eternal salvation. The same is true, incidentally, of a poem written some ten years later upon the death of a young daughter of one Johann Georg Dietrich von Burgk,[7] in which the poet logically argues the foolishness of grief and the good fortune of the child in having died so young. How effective such a consolation may be in the concrete case is perhaps open to some doubt.

A poem dedicated in 1642 to his teacher Christioph Köler, though conventional in its compliments and enthusiastic hyperboles,[8] does shed some light upon Scheffler's educational experience and his own scholarly temperament. In sixty lines, rhymed in pairs in the ubiquitous Alexandrine form, Scheffler thanks Köler for having led him out of the night of ignorance and compares the things he has learned from his teacher, interestingly enough, to the newly discovered treasures of America. Scheffler then goes on to say, in terms calculated to please any teacher, "My goal is knowledge and the favor of such people/who are like you" (ll. 38–39). Then, with the help of an eclectic battery of classical allusions, Scheffler turns to praise of the German language and its potentialities for literary greatness, a passage which must accurately reflect an important feature of the atmosphere in his school. Another poem of 1642, a hymn of praise entitled "Bonus consilarius" and addressed to an official of the Duchy of Brieg named

Andreas Lange von Langenau,[9] is noteworthy chiefly for its rather wearying length of 352 lines. With its assertion of the poet's own incompetence in the face of the nobleman's great magnificence and its tone of sycophantic hyperbole, it belongs to a vast genre of Baroque poems, very few of which can be confronted by the modern reader with anything but irritation. The only other evidence we have of Scheffler's participation in literary activities in his school consists of three accounts of literary recitations, among which was a May festival in 1642 in which Scheffler represented a nightingale.[10]

III   *University Years*

In the spring of 1643 Scheffler left the *Gymnasium* and matriculated to the University of Strassburg to study medicine. Of his experiences there we know nothing; and in any case he remained only one year, possibly because the professor to whom Köler had particularly recommended him happened to be away at that time.[11] In the summer of 1644 he transferred to the famous University of Leiden, and although we know nearly as little about his activities there as in Strassburg, there can be little doubt that Leiden was the second decisive educational experience in his life, for at Leiden he could not help being exposed to religious influences of the utmost importance for his development. Despite recurrent occasional lapses, Holland was on the whole the most tolerant country in Europe in matters of religion. It was natural, therefore, that the religious outcasts of the other nations should congregate there in considerable numbers. Jews there enjoyed relatively peaceful circumstances, and various Christian sectarians, who were under heavy attack from Catholics, Lutherans, and Calvinists alike, migrated to Holland. Among these groups were a number of a type that included the Mennonites (the ancestors of the Amish and Mennonites still found today in Pennsylvania, Ohio, and elsewhere in North America). The outstanding characteristics of these people were their relative indifference to structural church organization and their lively interest in the mystical tradition and the personal religion of the heart. Amsterdam was in fact the publishing center of European mysticism. Particularly the works of Jakob Böhme were in wide circulation.

The extent of Scheffler's interest in the mystical groups in Holland has been a subject of considerable debate carried on in an almost total vacuum of information. It is not even known, for instance, whether Scheffler ever visited Amsterdam. Scheffler himself contributed substantially to our difficulties in this matter. In 1664, when his pamphlet war was in full career, his major opponent, Johann Adam Schertzer, accused him of having associated with the Anabaptists while in Holland, a crime as serious in Lutheran as in Catholic eyes. Scheffler replied: "I was two years in Leiden, and to this hour I do not know where a Mennonite or Anabaptist church is to be found." [12] The awkwardness of this reply did not escape Schertzer, because it was well-known that the sectarians did not have churches, but gathered in conventicles.[13] It did therefore seem to be an evasive answer, and Scheffler never cleared the question up. Then and later Scheffler's relationship to the works of Jakob Böhme was also a matter of dispute. In the preface to the *Cherubinic Wanderer* (1657), he mentions a number of mystical figures who had influenced him, but the absence of any Protestants, as well as of Eckhart, who had been placed on the Index, and particularly of Böhme, is conspicuous.[14] Schertzer, however, reported that Scheffler had presented his assistant with a copy of Böhme's *Aurora* accompanied by a strong recommendation.[15]

This dispute would not interest us much today if it had not been revived in the modern debate upon Scheffler's actual religious position and the specific influences which formed it. Those who have attempted, against all odds, to claim complete Catholic orthodoxy for Scheffler's poetry tend to take him at his word in his introduction and to discount the Protestant attacks as mere polemical mendacity.[16] Although it is true that the reliablity of Scheffler's opponents is open to some doubt, Schertzer in this case does give the impression of being very well informed. On the other hand, given Scheffler's later development, and the fact that he was in Holland at a time when there is no evidence that he was at all interested in Catholicism, it is all but impossible that he did not occupy himself with the Protestant mystical tradition and with Jakob Böhme in particular, both in Holland and also in the early 1650's. Anyone not attempting to construct a hagiography of Scheffler will find it easier to believe that, in his introduction of 1657, the newly formed Catholic fanatic found it more appropriate to suppress the Protestant and sectarian influences which had concerned him in earlier days. In any case, the whole argument is not entirely pertinent, as we shall see when we examine the *Cherubinic Wanderer.*

On the basis of Scheffler's own testimony, it appears that he left Leiden in the fall of 1646.[17] He now drops out of sight for about a year, during which time there is some evidence that he traveled in southern Germany and in Italy.[18] On September 25, 1647, he matriculated at the University of Padua, a natural step for him, as Padua was famous for medicine; and he recieved a combined M.D. and Ph.D. on July 9, 1648.[19] At this point Scheffler again drops out of sight for about a year, but it seems probable that he returned to Breslau, at least partly for family reasons.[20] During this whole period nothing is known of his personal life and interests. His later account that his interest in Catholicism developed during his travels through Catholic cities[21] must be viewed with some caution, in view of the actual circumstances of his conversion. It may be a reinterpretation of his later years. Only a single document gives a hint of his state of mind during this time: In a letter of 1649 he makes the observation, *mundus pulcherrimum nihil*—"the world is a most beautiful naught."[22] The phrase suggests a tension in Scheffler's mind between a sensual appreciation of the material beauty of the world and an intellectual and religious conviction of its futility and meaninglessness. If so, it may mark a final stage in his development, because in his later writings there are only rare traces of an appreciation of the beauty of creation.

IV *Friendship with Franckenberg*

The next step in Scheffler's life provides another reason against assuming any serious interest in Catholicism at so early a period. In June, 1649, he was appointed court physician to the ruler of the principality of Oels in Silesia, Duke Sylvius Nimrod of Württemberg (1622–64). Sylvius Nimrod was an energetic and strictly orthodox Lutheran prince, whom Scheffler could not possibly have served had he then been in the religious mood which characterized his later years. Furthermore, although this position was to turn out badly, there is no evidence that at any point Scheffler got into difficulties with Sylvius Nimrod himself. His connections then indicate rather that his religious attitude was not bound by any of the churches and that his interest was moving in a mystical direction characteristically indifferent to denominational allegiances. For at this time we see Scheffler connected to an important personage with all the loyalty and devotion of which his dependent personality was capable.

Abraham von Franckenberg (1593–1652) was a wealthy nobleman with exclusively spiritual and intellectual interests. In his youth he had transferred his property to his brother, and he lived as an ascetic in an apartment of his own ancestral castle. He developed a considerable reputation for selfless deeds, especially during the plague of 1634.[23] Because of difficulties with the Lutheran clergy and the troubles of the war, he left his home in 1645 for Danzig, where he boarded with the famous mathematician Helvelius. He returned home in 1650 and died in June, 1652. Franckenberg had a variety of interests, including alchemy, the Cabbala, and the heretical philosophy of Giordano Bruno, who had been burned at the stake in 1600, but he is best remembered for his devotion to Jakob Böhme. The erudite nobleman placed himself at the feet of the self-taught visionary shoemaker and did much to bring his writings into circulation. He published an edition of Böhme in Danzig in 1642. Franckenberg was not a man to be bound by the distinctions between organized denominations. It is reported that when Sylvius Nimrod asked him what his religion was, he replied, "I am the heart (COR) of religions, i.e., Catholic, Orthodox, Reformed." [24]

Scheffler's acquaintance with Franckenberg cannot have begun before 1650, when the latter returned to Silesia from Danzig, and can at most have lasted some two years until Franckenberg's death on June 25, 1652. There can be no doubt that the men were strongly attracted to one another and that Scheffler received much inspiration from the relationship, particularly in connection with the mystical tradition. Before he died, Franckenberg presented Scheffler with a copy of a book containing sermons of Johannes Tauler (ca. 1300–1361) and the visions of St. Mechthild (ca. 1207–83) and St. Gertrude (1256–1302), as well as an edition of the revelations of St. Bridget of Sweden (ca. 1300–1375) bound together with a volume by Heinrich Suso (ca. 1295–1366).[25] When Franckenberg died, he left the remainder of his library to Scheffler; and although we do not know its exact contents, what we can ascertain of Franckenberg's reading suggests that it contained a wide variety of mystical and occult writings, including Ruysbroeck (1293–1381), the so-called *Theologia Deutsch* (before 1400), Thomas à Kempis (*ca.* 1380–1471), Böhme, Valentin Weigel (1533–89), Sebastian Franck (1499–1542), the Rosicrucian Johann Valentin Andreae (1586–1654), Paracelsus, and others.[26]

Franckenberg had a circle of friends some of whom also seemed to have been acquainted with Scheffler. The mystic poet Johann Theodor von Tschesch (1595–1649), who wrote religious epigrams in Latin, may have died before Scheffler got to know him; but it is known that Franckenberg possessed his manuscripts,[27] and it is therefore likely that Scheffler saw them. Of the greatest importance was his probable acquaintance with the work of the religious writer and poet Daniel Czepko von Reigersfeld (1605–60), of whom we will have more to say in the chapter on the *Cherubinic Wanderer*. Scheffler also came to know Georg Betke,[28] who supported his brother Joachim, a Protestant preacher, in a campaign against the orthodox Lutheran establishment. Betke accused the Lutherans of hypocrisy and of indifference to Christ's qualities of humility and to his Passion. He made them responsible for the decay of religious life and the atrocities of the war and argued an "essential Christianity" against what he regarded as the bibliolatry of the official Lutheran position. These arguments may well have made an impression on Scheffler, for they recur, appropriately adjusted, in his own apology after his conversion.

Franckenberg's death in 1652 was a heavy blow to Scheffler, who badly needed a warm and inspirational friendship of this kind. For some reason, possibly because of difficulties with the Lutheran clergy, Franckenberg's funeral was not held until November 14, five months after his death, on which occasion Scheffler wrote a eulogy, "Christian Memorial of Honor for Herr Abraham von Franckenberg," [29] the first work we know of Scheffler's in which his poetic gifts begin to be evident—inspired, no doubt, by the sincerity of his grief. The poem consists of twenty-eight four-line stanzas in rhymed Alexandrine pairs, of which the first pair has a feminine rhyme and the second a masculine, that is, twelve and thirteen syllables, respectively. What is striking about the poem, aside from its power of expression, is the unmistakable appearance of mystical concepts. Scheffler does not hesitate to express the unity with God which Franckenberg has achieved in the radical manner characteristic of the *Cherubinic Wanderer:* "You are a God with God" (1. 23). The final stanza could easily have appeared in the later work:

> Wer Zeit nimmt ohne Zeit und Sorgen ohne Sorgen,
> Wem gestern war wie heut und heute gilt wie morgen,
> Wer alles gleiche schätzt,—*der* tritt schon in der Zeit
> In den gewünschten Stand der lieben Ewigkeit.

> (Whoever accepts time without time and cares without care,
> For whom yesterday was like today and today is the same as
>   tomorrow,
> Whoever estimates all things alike, he enters already in time,
> Into the desired state of dear eternity.)

The combination of a quietistic approach to this world with the possibility of achieving the experience of eternity even in earthly time is one of the major themes of the later work.

V *The Conversion*

It is surely no accident that Scheffler began to get into difficulties almost immediately after Franckenberg's death and that he began to move in the direction of a new kind of dependence. Sometime in 1652 Scheffler decided to put together a collection of mystical prayers, including some by St. Gertrude, as a present for his friends. In order to do this, he had to submit the manuscript to the chaplain of the court of Oels, a zealous Lutheran named Christoph Freytag, with whom Franckenberg and his circle had apparently already had difficulties. The Lutheran clergy had come to take a dim view of mysticism because of its obvious centrifugal tendencies. The Lutherans, finding themselves under increasing pressure from the Counter Reformation, and threatened within the Protestant camp by the followers of Calvin, of Schwenkfeld, and of other sects, felt that their best defense lay in maintaining unity of organization and dogma. Consequently the mystics, with their indifference to these matters, were scorned as "enthusiasts," and especially the followers of Jakob Böhme were in bad odor with the Lutheran establishment of Silesia. So it was that Christoph Freytag refused to permit the publication of Scheffler's book. Censorship was a fact of life in the seventeenth century, and another man might have swallowed his disappointment and let the matter pass. But Scheffler had been attacked at what had come to be the central interest in his spiritual life. If the official Lutheran establishment was determined to suppress the expression of mystical experience, how was he to continue to live under their authority? Scheffler wrote to Georg Betke on November 28, 1652, with great bitterness: "He [Freytag] does not let me discuss them [the prayers] with a single word, but writes on them: 'These prayers cannot be printed, so that His Princely Grace and the priesthood in the city as well as in the country shall not expose themselves to the suspicion that they want to support the enthusiasts.' And sends it to the printer like that, even though the names of the authors were written over every poem. What sort of priestly judgment and apostolical procedure this is, I leave to anyone to decide. From now on I know exactly what I should think of them." [30]

Just when Scheffler began to consider seriously conversion to Catholicism is not known. His Catholic apologists like to minimize the importance of the clash with Freytag in this process; others see in that event evidence that Scheffler's mystical interests were nondenominational and that he made the change only when he could no longer pursue those interests within the Lutheran Church. This argument is mostly based on speculation. But it should be noted that Scheffler's bitter account of the affair was sent to a *Protestant*, although a dissenting one; and the chronology of events suggest quite clearly that his frustration at the hands of Freytag was at least the last, decisive straw. By December, 1652, Scheffler no longer held his position at the strictly Lutheran court of Oels.[31] Just when he left it is not known. Half a year later, on June 12, 1653, Scheffler was converted to Roman Catholicism in the Church of Saint Matthew in Breslau, taking the name Johann Angelus.[32]

In view of the lively debate concerning the motives of this step, which has continued in the literature on Scheffler, it perhaps would be safest to say that it is possible he was not altogether clear in his own mind about the consequences of it. It is likely that Scheffler was already writing parts of the *Cherubinic Wanderer* at this time; and despite monumental efforts to the contrary, it is not possible to turn that work into an orthodox Catholic document. Perhaps there was a stage in the process when Scheffler actually did think that a denominationally indifferent mysticism would be freer from authoritarian interference in the Catholic Church. If so, however, he reckoned without two important considerations: the fact that in the circumstances, such a step on the part of a gifted and rather highly placed person would thrust him *nolens volens* into a prominent position in the bitter Silesian Counter Reformation; and, more importantly, his own need for loyal and loving dependence, now that the great object of his devotion was dead, would bring him very quickly into total subservience to the new authority. This feature of the situation appeared quite promptly in the defense of his action which he felt obliged to publish shortly after his conversion.

Scheffler's *Fundamental Causes and Motives Why he Left Lutheranism and Professed the Catholic Church* (printed separately in Olmütz and Ingolstadt, 1653)[33] was called forth by the stir which his conversion had caused. (In view of the fact that conversions back and forth were taking place every day in these unsettled times, the fuss seems to indicate that Scheffler was already regarded as a person of some consequence.) The document does not seem very extraordinary at first glance. The arguments presented are those of the Catholic side in a debate the terms of which had remained almost unaltered since the beginning of the Reformation polemic in the 1520's; and, indeed, throughout Scheffler's polemical career there is nothing on either side of the battle that contributes any substantially new ideas to this interminable theological standoff. A closer reading, however, shows that Scheffler's placing of accents and stresses is revealing, particularly in the order in which he makes his points. Of the twenty aspects of Lutheranism Scheffler finds unacceptable, the major theological issue, justification by faith alone, stands only in tenth place. The first four points, however, are briefly as follows: (1) The newness of the doctrine; (2) the arbitrary Protestant exegesis of the Word of God without regard to tradition; (3) the frivolity of Luther's character and his tendency to contradict himself; (4) the disunity within the Protestant camp on points of doctrine. It is clear that the issue of *certainty* is in the foreground. The Lutherans, with their lack of tradition, their denial of the Church as the incarnation of the Holy Ghost, their internal dissensions, and their willingness to listen to what Scheffler was later to call "the idol of reason," simply frightened him. The defense of Catholicism, which he appended here to his criticism of the Lutherans, turns in large part on the comforting effect of the long-unbroken tradition. These themes run through all of Scheffler's prose writings until the end of his life. Many students of Scheffler have wondered how a man with the mystical vision expressed so extraordinarily in the *Cherubinic Wanderer* could have become a fanatical, ruthless, dogmatically bound agent of the Counter Reformation. The answer is to be found, at least in part, in his own account of himself at this moment in his life. The courage, the individuality, and the expansive intellectual and spiritual imagination required of the mystic, though present in Scheffler, were not strong enough to counteract his need to subordinate himself in loyalty, devotion, and admiration. He had attached himself to Franckenberg much to the benefit of his spiritual well-being. After Franckenberg died, Scheffler lost little time in yielding purposefully to a new authority. It may fairly be questioned whether Scheffler's second, and final, loyalty brought him rewards of equal quality.

Scheffler's *Fundamental Causes* was not a polemic written in his later style but a quiet-spoken personal confession in rather measured tones. One of his great opponents, the Jena professor Christian Chemnitz, replied two years later with a sharp pamphlet,[34] but Scheffler did not answer. His mind, as we shall see presently, was better occupied elsewhere. Moreover, at this time, as apparently throughout most of his life, he seems to have devoted a good portion of his energies to the medical profession. On March 24, 1654, Emperor Ferdinand III appointed him Royal Imperial Court Physician,[35] a purely honorary title with no emolument, so that it cannot have been, as his enemies charged, the bribe for his conversion. It is more likely that it was a recognition of his accomplishments as a physician. Of Scheffler's other activities in the mid-1650's we know little, but it must have been in these years that he caught the attention of Sebastian von Rostock (1607–71), who at that time was vicar general and chief agent of the Counter Reformation in Breslau and later (1664) became Prince-Bishop. It is with Rostock in mind that Flitch writes of Scheffler: "Of him it may be said that there were friends by whom he was saved and friends from whom the pity of it was that he could not be saved." [36] Franckenberg was one of the former, and Rostock was surely one of the latter. This artisan's son, by reason of his energy, intelligence, single-mindedness, and nearly proverbial courage, had risen to be one of the major exponents of the Counter Reformation in Silesia. Tales of his rough-and-ready character circulated in the land, among them the story that once, upon being beset by robbers, he ran one of them through and then immediately leaped from his horse to give his victim the last rites. His major occupation became the aggressive recovery of churches and other property from the Protestants, property to which the Catholic Church was entitled under the terms of the Treaty of Westphalia, but the recovery of which was not without its difficulties, for the population was at that time noticeably unenthusiastic about the re-Catholicization of Silesia. It is more than likely that the alert Rostock quickly sensed the possibilities which lay in Scheffler's combination of a gift for writing with his willingness to support the cause absolutely. If it is at all true that Scheffler at the time of his conversion was not prepared to go the whole way to Catholic fanaticism, then it was undoubtedly Rostock who conducted him the remaining distance.

VI *The Poet Emerges*

Rostock, like Freytag, was a censor. An important step in his cultivation of Scheffler was the imprimatur which he gave to two poetical works published in 1657, the books which have come to be known as the *Cherubinic Wanderer* and *Heilige Seelenlust* (*Holy Joy of the Soul*), both published under the name of Angelus Silesius. The latter work, which, as we shall see, belongs to a tradition cultivated by the Jesuits, was published in Breslau; but the former, Scheffler's masterpiece, was published in Vienna, apparently through the mediation of another prominent Catholic writer, the Jesuit Nicolaus Avancinus (1612–86).[37] The interpretation placed upon these events by those critics who are not concerned with proving Scheffler's consistent Catholic orthodoxy seems irresistible in its logic. It is, briefly, as follows: Rostock must have known that Scheffler had received a jolt from the Lutheran establishment by its refusal to allow his harmless mystical book to be printed, and he did not want to alienate the valuable confederate by suppressing the less harmless *Cherubinic Wanderer*. Therefore he compromised by having it printed about as far away from Breslau as possible, in cosmopolitan Vienna, whereas the more tolerable *Holy Joy of the Soul* could appear on the premises without any difficulty. This seems to have been the curious way in which Scheffler's two major works saw the light of day.

The genesis of these two works is not known. It is not even clear which is earlier. All we know about them is that Scheffler claimed to have written the 302 poems and couplets of the first book of the *Cherubinic Wanderer* in a four-day wave of inspiration,[38] but we do not know when. On the basis of internal evidence and the dates which circumscribe the influence of Franckenberg and Czepko, Ellinger has argued that the first two books of the *Cherubinic Wanderer* were probably written in 1651; the third book in 1652, when Scheffler was interested in St. Gertrude and St. Mechthild; and the fourth and fifth, which show more Catholic influence, around the time of his difficulties with Christoph Freytag in late 1652 or early 1653.[39] Also for reasons of content Ellinger places the more orthodox *Holy Joy of the Soul* somewhat later.[40] These arguments make sense, but any student of modern literary theory will recognize that arguments from content can yield nothing more than an intelligent guess; in fact we do not know just when in the period from 1651 to 1657 the works were written.

VII *Agent of the Counter Reformation*

From this time until around 1660 Scheffler's activities are not known. The result demonstrates, however, that during this time he was deepening his commitment to a particularly ascetic form of Catholicism. In 1660 we begin, once more, to have records of him that indicate quite clearly the direction in which his religious commitment was carrying him. We have evidence of considerable charitable activity. Scheffler made a number of gifts to the Church to provide for special rituals and apparently also stood godfather to a number of poor children.[41] It must be said, incidentally, that Scheffler's professed disdain for worldly things was undoubtedly genuine. He seems to have unburdened himself of his entire moderate fortune for charitable purposes. A more curious aspect of his activity is his interest in public processions, which had been forbidden in Breslau since the Reformation, and which both he and Rostock endeavored on several occasions to reinstitute as part of the reconstruction of Catholic prestige in Silesia. A memorandum by Scheffler, dated July 9, 1660, refers to his intentions in one of these processions, and is worth transmitting here in full because it is the single most instructive document from this period of his life:

1. I wish to carry the cross through the city with a crown on my head so that I may become like Christ who carried the Cross through the city with the Crown of Thorns on his most sacred head. 2. So that I may thank Christ in word and deed that he carried the Cross for my sake. 3. So that I will be dishonored before all and despised by all, for I am worthy of that, and Christ was dishonored and despised before me. Furthermore, the greater part will call me a fool or consider me greedy for honor, as though by doing this I were seeking some vain glory; and thus I will lose much of the esteem in which I was previously held. 4. So that I may serve as an example of devotion to all the pious. 5. So that I will serve the conversion of the city, and of all those who shall laugh at me, which is my particular intention.[42]

The naïve combination of tense self-abnegation with an almost insuperable *hubris* reflected in this document requires no comment. One may note, however, the characteristic illogicality and lack of psychological sensitivity in the last sentence—Scheffler always had very strange views on how conversions might actually be achieved—as well as the anachronistic medieval quality of this kind of asceticism, which is an indication of the conflict into which Scheffler was to come with the spirit of his own time. Another procession in Breslau, probably in 1662, was to cause Scheffler some grief because his enemies spread stories that he had slipped and fallen in the mud while carrying the monstrance with the consecrated Host. Scheffler disputed this warmly, and Schertzer's defense of the story is so weak that it may not be true at all.[43] It is an example, however, of the level of public debate in the atmosphere of that time.

In May, 1661, Scheffler took a further and not very surprising step: He was ordained a priest. Contrary to some rumors, he never joined an order, although he had close connections to the

Third Order of St. Francis and apparently also to the Jesuits, which is again not surprising. Scheffler's patron, Sebastian von Rostock, had been instrumental in smuggling the Jesuits into Silesia while they were still illegal and had encouraged their activities afterward. Scheffler's polemical efforts were carried on in the spirit of the Jesuits and seem to have been influenced by one of the great Jesuit battlers of the time, Jodocus Kedd (1597–1655). In 1664 the redoubtable Rostock became Prince-Bishop of Breslau and quickly appointed Scheffler his court marshal. This rather worldly post seems a curious position for Scheffler to have been in, and he probably found little pleasure in it. In 1666, on the occasion of a disagreement with an official of the court, Scheffler, who according to a friendly anonymous account[44] could have settled the dispute with a few words, instead took the opportunity to resign.

VIII *The Polemicist*

Meanwhile, he had opened his polemical career with a thunderous explosion in 1663. In the summer of that year the Turks began what for the moment appeared to be a dangerous advance in Hungary, seriously threatening Moravia and Silesia. This phase of the tenacious Turkish offensive against the powers of Central Europe had been going on since 1645, but the Turkish threat generally had a history reaching well back into the sixteenth century. In 1521 the Turks had taken Belgrad and in 1526 the capital of Hungary. Three years later they began the first siege of Vienna itself. What Scheffler noticed was that these were precisely the years when Luther's Reformation began to spread through the religious and political life of Germany. Now the Old Testament provides an extremely pervasive argument to the effect that the political and military defeat of God's people at the hands of the heathen is a divine punishment for faithlessness. Scheffler's by now thoroughly dogmatic mind drew a conclusion almost frightening in its simplicity: In a pamphlet published on October 29, 1663, entitled *Turkish Pamphlet of the Causes of the Turkish Invasion and the Downtreading of the People of God,* he argued that the Turks represented God's punishment for the Reformation and the continuing disloyalty to the Roman Catholic Church.

We will turn our attention more closely to the contents of this and others of Scheffler's polemical writings in our final chapter. Here it is important to note that the publication of this pamphlet represented another crucial turning point in his career. Scheffler's argument touched a whole bundle of raw nerves, and there was a swift reaction of shock and anger. On February 8, 1664, the city of Magdeburg demanded in the Imperial Diet that the emperor punish Scheffler, and this proposal was supported not only by the Protestants but also by the Catholic bishops of Salzburg, Paderborn, Trent, and Münster. While the proposal does not seem to have carried—nothing was done, in any case—the handwriting on the wall was plain. After a century and a half, Germany was beginning to weary of religious strife. The Thirty Years' War had raped the land but solved little. The weakened Empire was beset by the intrigues and aggressions of France in the west and the formidable Turkish threat to the east. New political ideas began to show themselves here and there, among them the possibility that the Empire could continue indefinitely part Protestant and part Catholic, and, indeed, the revolutionary possibility that the state could tolerate the existence of competing religious organizations without demanding absolute confessional unity. That such ideas had gained a little ground is the only explanation for the stand taken by some Catholic bishops against the Catholic polemicist Scheffler. Under the circumstances he appeared as a major troublemaker. At this point Scheffler was faced with a decision. The signs of Catholic opposition to his fanaticism were a suggestion to him to moderate his public actions. But Scheffler was not a moderate man. Wholehearted, uncompromising subordination was an overwhelming need of his personality. His decision was to continue on the road he had begun to take. Scheffler started his journey into isolation.

The polemical style of the religious schism in Germany was introduced by Martin Luther himself as well as by his opponents. Luther's style, which is usually apostrophized by his admirers as soundly popular and healthy, is often simply crude and vulgar, reflecting the intolerance of an unsubtle and single-minded man. But there is another side to it, to be sure. The rough and homely but always exact and sometimes highly poetic style and cadence of Luther's German produced a Bible translation which is one of the immortal achievements of world literature, and his polemics are intelligent, richly argued, and usually very much to the point. By the seventeenth century, however, the terms of the whole dispute had worn thin. What remained was largely a method of angry hammer blows with dogmatic propositions and a vast but unedifying vocabulary of *ad hominem* insult and defamation. In the pamphlets which flew back and forth in the 1660's and 1670's, Scheffler on the whole makes the better impression. His argumentation is more cogent than that of his opponents, his reliance upon vituperation less, his pertinence more consistent; and, above all, he writes better. Rarely does Scheffler put down a sentence which does not yield its meaning at first reading, whereas his opponents, particularly Johann Adam Schertzer, write German as though the literary development of the century had never taken place. On the other hand, from any modern point of view, Scheffler's purposes are discouraging: In 1665 he attacked the reliance placed on reason by the Lutherans and Calvinists;[45] in 1666 he argued the sovereignty of the Pope of Rome over the Germans;[46] in 1667 he attacked the Lutheran claim of being able to demonstrate their religion from Scripture, arguing, among other things, that no salvation outside the Church was possible and that religion as such existed only within the Church and its interpretations.[47] So it went, year after year, and the worst was yet to come.

In 1671 Sebastian von Rostock was still energetically laboring at the reclamation of Catholic Church property, an effort which naturally brought him into conflict with Scheffler's patron of former days, Sylvius Nimrod. In a dispute over benefices with Sylvius Nimrod, the Emperor decided against Rostock, putting the bishop into such a fury that he died of a stroke on June 6. Once again Scheffler seems to have taken his loss hard; Ellinger argues that the event may have convinced Scheffler that even the best of heretics, such as Sylvius Nimrod, were tools of Satan and must be met with force.[48] Perhaps so. In any case, Scheffler again lost no time in finding a new master to whom he could subordinate himself, an abbot in Grüssau named Bernhard Rosa who had captured Scheffler's attention by eradicating Protestantism in his parish without much attention to finer sensibilities. As early as 1670, Scheffler had written a pamphlet in which he suggested that the legal rights of Protestants in Silesia should be abrogated because they had departed in some points from the terms of the Augsburg

Confession.[49] It is no wonder that his enemies occasionally accused him of sedition. Now, in 1673, came the stunning climax of the whole series, a long pamphlet the tone of which is sufficiently indicated by its title: *Coercion of Conscience Justified, or Proof That One Can and Should Force the Heretics to the True Faith.* The ultimate sum of the doctrine that error has no rights had been drawn.

Scheffler claims to have written fifty-five polemic and didactic tracts between 1663 and 1675.[50] In 1677 he collected thirty-nine of them and published them, after considerable revision, under the title *Ecclesiologia,* in which the various writings combine into a mighty apology for the Church and a powerful defense against the heretics. Although a second edition was published in Oberammergau in 1735, the world by and large shrugged it off, and even the Jesuits appear not to have been particularly enthusiastic about it. Meanwhile, Scheffler published some other things in his later years. In 1668 he put out a second edition of the *Holy Joy of the Soul,* with an additional fifth book, and in 1674 a long four-part poem, *Sensual Description of the Four Last Things to the Wholesome Terror and Encouragement of All Men,* to which we shall devote a brief chapter below. The following year a new edition of the *Cherubinic Wanderer* appeared, bearing the title by which it was to be known to posterity, and also expanded by an additional book. In 1676, Scheffler published a translation of a mystical work, *Margarita Evangelica,* to which he gave the title *The Precious Evangelical Pearl for the Complete Ornamentation of the Bride of Christ.* The Latin *Margarita evangelica,* published in 1545, was a translation of the original Dutch version of 1539, the authorship of which is not clear, but it may have been written by a Dutch nun in the neo-Catholic mystical tradition. Ellinger remarks that the smoothness and skill with which Scheffler carried off this project proves what he might have achieved as a prose writer had he been able to discipline his temperament.[51] A Latin work about John the Evangelist, mentioned in the eulogy at Scheffler's funeral, has never been found.[52]

IX *The Final Pathos*

Under the pressure of his asceticism, his loneliness, and his labors, Scheffler's health had long been weakened. He spent his last years living in the cloister of the church in which he had converted and was probably tubercular. His melancholy personal remarks in the preface to the *Ecclesiologia* are the words not only of a dying man, but also of one who has not found contentment. He speaks in a moving way of the hatred, persecution, and slander by which he was surrounded, without, however, considering the extent to which he himself was responsible for this situation. In his quaint way he describes also his isolation from those Catholics "who out of lack of love would allow the heretics to go quietly and peacefully to Hell rather than anger them with the truth." [53] In the same year, on July 9, 1677, the twenty-ninth anniversary of his doctor's degree, Scheffler died at the age of fifty-two, after having spent the weeks of his last illness in isolated meditation. On the occasion of his funeral, a Jesuit priest named Daniel Schwartz delivered a eulogy, subsequently published,[54] in which he praises Scheffler's Christian virtues, his selfless charity, and his activities as a physician with uncommon warmth, and in the heavy, learned, but passionate style of the time compares him to the angels. Nowhere does he mention either the *Cherubinic Wanderer* or the *Ecclesiologia*.

It is a dubious undertaking to pass judgment upon the vision and the yearnings of a man from another age. But it is understandable that the life of Johann Scheffler has been regarded as largely a wasted one. Passionate and aggressive, but also easily wounded and sensitive, and incurably dependent besides, he permitted his great gifts as poet and visionary to be submerged in a victory of the intellect over his qualities of soul. Harsh as it may sound, it is a temptation to say that Scheffler did not have the strength to respond to his vocation, but instead chose a simpler and easier one which made him an anachronism in his own time and, in a sense, thereby obliterated him as a person. For it is not the name of Johann Scheffler which is cherished in the memory of men. History has separated from that total personality the literary name Angelus Silesius under which he published his poetry; and it is as Angelus Silesius that he will be remembered in the history of German poetry. To his poetic achievement we must now turn.

CHAPTER 2

Masterpiece: The Cherubinic Wanderer

I *Introduction*

THE book we now know as the *Cherubinic Wanderer* contains 1,676 poems divided into six books. Of these, ten are sonnets, and the bulk of the remainder are rhymed Alexandrine couplets, although a few number four, six, or eight lines, and one (VI, 11) is as long as twenty-eight lines. The fame of the work, however, rests almost exclusively upon the rhymed couplets. The first edition of the work, which contained only the first five books with the ten sonnets appended, appeared in 1657 under the title *Geist-reiche Sinn- und Schluss-reime* (*Sagacious Rhyming Sentences and Epigrams*). The title *Cherubinischer Wandersmann* was added to the second edition, which was published in 1675 and contained the additional sixth book, headed by the ten sonnets. The reference to the Cherubim in this title may require some explanation, because the meaning of the word has been obscured in modern usage. In the mythological hierarchy of the heavenly hosts, the Cherubim are the second order of angels, whose attribute is knowledge. The first order is that of the Seraphim, the angels of love and devotion. Thus, the adjective "Cherubinic" fits the sense of the rather pretentious original title and underscores the sharply intellectual quality of this work and of the mysticism from which it is derived. In this way Scheffler makes a clear distinction from the Seraphic element, the mysticism of love-service, which predominates in the lyrical *Holy Joy of the Soul.* As for the "Wanderer," the word may simply suggest a pilgrim, although it must be said that the work wanders in another sense: it is impossible to extract any significant structure from the order and arrangement of the poems in the book.

It is not known when any part of the *Cherubinic Wanderer* was written. Arguments from internal evidence are made uncertain by the lack of thematic organization and by our vague knowledge of the stages in Scheffler's spiritual progress. In his preface Scheffler says nothing about the genesis of the work except that the verses were written "for the most part without premeditation and laborious reflection in a short time" and that he "completed the first book in four days." [1] A careful reading seems to indicate that the first two books most consistently reflect the extra-denominational attitudes of the Franckenberg circle, whereas beginning wih the third book there are themes which are more specifically Catholic. Consequently, Scheffler's conversion in 1653 is usually taken as a *terminus ad quem* by those who attempt to date the work; the *terminus a quo* is almost certainly Scheffler's acquaintance with Czepko's *Sexcenta monodisticha sapientium* through Franckenberg around 1651.[2] The dating arguments are speculation at best, however, and it is not quite clear, if these limits are correct, why it took Scheffler four years to publish the work even though he had removed himself from the authority of Christoph Freytag by his conversion. Another difficulty is that the fifth book, by far the longest, with its 374 verses, overcomes some of the slackness evident in Book III and especially Book IV, and reverts to the more consistent daring of the first two, an observation which confounds any certain attempt to tie the genesis of the work to Scheffler's development in those years. For the sixth book, which is on the whole more obviously Catholic than the others, and also less accomplished, there is similarly no evidence; but given the usual speed of publication in the seventeenth century, there is no reason to think that it was not written immediately before it was published in 1675.

The *Cherubinic Wanderer* is not a creation *ex nihilo*. Unique as it is as a total achievement, it is dependent upon traditions which nourished it. It will be necessary to look at least briefly at those traditions before examining some aspects of the work itself.

II *The Mystical Tradition*

> Carven gods long gone . . .
>   Dead leaves alone foregather
> On the temple porch.[3]

So reads the English translation of a *haiku* by Basho (1644–94). The *haiku* is the characteristic verse form of the mystical Zen sect of Japanese Buddhism that some years ago began to play a part in a complicated effort at spiritual renewal among young Americans. The example, apparently so far afield, is in fact relevant to the subject at hand for several reasons, and not only because it is nearly contemporaneous with the *Cherubinic Wanderer*. For one thing, mysticism is encountered just about everywhere in the great religious traditions of the world, East and West. And although it would be futile to deny that there are significant differences between various kinds of mystical phenomena, some of its basic characteristics show a striking similarity in widely separated ages and cultures. Secondly, it is a phenomenon which apparently refuses to die; and it has a way of flourishing at times when institutionalized faiths and dogmas fail to meet the anxieties of human existence, as the experimentations of the "Beatniks" have proven once more. Finally, it is in the nature of mysticism that it should often be connected with noteworthy literary achievement. Mysticism, like poetry, attempts to escape from the conceptual rationalism enforced by the ordinary use of language and to expand the ability of language to direct attention beyond its boundaries into the realm of the inexpressible. This last point connects the *haiku* with the verses of Angelus Silesius in a quite important way.

Mysticism is a vast topic and virtually defies comprehensive definition. It is not even helpful to ask what mysticism is about, for, as David Baumgardt has pointed out, its topics are often the same as those of metaphysics, religion, or even science. The difference is one of approach, which in mysticism is synthetic and intuitive, "a species of divination." [4] Its characteristic is the effort at union between the subject and the object of knowledge, the renowned *unio mystica,* which often is, but need not necessarily be, an effort for total and utter union with the substances of God. William James, in his Edinburg lectures on the varieties of religious experience (1901–2), isolates four qualities which help one to approach the nature of this kind of experience. They are ineffability, the noetic quality, transiency, and passivity. [5] The first two of these, says James, are always present; the second two may or may not be. The quality of ineffability means, quite simply, that the matters of concern to the mystic are inexpressible and all but incommunicable. This is the great and fruitful paradox of mystical literature: a methodology for communicating that which is essentially inexpressible must somehow be found, the matter must be intimated, or suggested, or something must be done to make the reader susceptible to the transcendental notions which the mystic has already perceived but cannot reproduce without seriously distorting them. The noetic quality means that what the mystic feels to be true is known to him. He has no answer to the epistemological problem of how he knows and is, in fact, not concerned with it. He knows by revelation, and his knowing is beyond the boundaries of sense and reason, beyond the possibility of demonstration. Transiency refers to the individual mystical state or experience. There is a dreamlike quality about it. It does not last very long, and although it leaves an indelible impression, it is often difficult to recall in detail. This, James points out, is not necessarily the case; there have been mystics who have lived their lives in a state of trance, sometimes so profound that they have been incapable of performing any useful action whatsoever. But in general the mystical state is not an enduring one. By passivity is meant the fact that the mystical state is most often not something achieved but something that happens. It is produced by a power other than the self. This quality is even less universal than the quality of transiency. Certainly the ministry of mystical preachers and poets would have no meaning if one could do nothing to make himself at least receptive to the experience; and, indeed, the careers and doctrines of many mystics include considerable attention to the *vita activa.*

The Christian mystical tradition has many roots, some of which go back to the mystery religions of Hellenic Greece. The word itself is derived from the Greek verb μύειν, which means to close the eyes and ears and shut the mouth. It is connected to the English word "mute." Other traditions come from the ancient Near East; and from the time of the Hellenized Jew, Philo of Alexandria (*ca.* 20 B.C.–*ca.* A.D. 50), who viewed God not as a concept but as a mystically experienced reality, there is a long and important Jewish tradition which has many points of tangency with Christian mysticism. However, as one attempts to think out the logic of Christian mystical teachings as they appear in their various guises, one finds oneself constantly confronting variations of the Neoplatonic doctrine of emanation, deriving from Plotinus (*ca.* 205–270). Stated roughly, the idea is that all creation is an emanation from God, the single unity in the universe—thrust out, as it were, from the substance of God to form a decreasing scale of reality—divine Mind, the world soul, particular souls, and, finally, material things. Consequently everything participates in God to a certain degree, but the lower orders of creation, by reason of their distance from the single unified source, less so. Thus the dualism between Creator and creation is considerably moderated, since everything is found to be on a relative scale; and although the mystic never tires of reasserting the vastness and distance of God beyond any human power to comprehend Him or assign attributes to Him, on the other hand there is an unbroken chain of being that connects all creatures with God. Indeed, the creatures participate to some degree in the Godhead, and thus the mystic, who is gifted with a strong sense of the possibilities inherent in this account of reality, becomes obsessed with the yearning to return into God, to reachieve the original union through what is sometimes called remanation, and, by submerging himself in God, to become his own unsullied true essence. The difficulty is that the creatures who are on the outer ends of this divine emanation differ from the original essence of God by their selfhood and individuation, the most notorious example of which is man's will. It is the will of the self-asserting individual, suffering and desiring, stubbornly maintaining its differentiation from the godhead, which stands between man and the mystical union. Thus the paradoxical imperative is that man should bend his will to its own destruction, neutralize his will, and empty out his inner self in order to achieve the ultimate union. Into the vacuum of the soul God will then flow; for it is found that there is as much longing on God's side as on man's for the ultimate reunion. Indeed, it is often boldly asserted in many ways that God means nothing without man and that it is precisely this mutual relationship of potential return which is the *raison d'être* of both God and man.

This relation of the mystical experience is, as I have said, roughly stated. Mystical doctrine appears in hundreds of refined variations. Often there is an element of visionary experience. The possibility of this blissful union is made certain in an experienced event, however brief. Furthermore, although it would seem that there is little room in the doctrine for ethical content, and indeed mysticism has often been accused by its detractors of ethical indifference, the fact is that ethical concerns and an attention to works appear with great stress in the writings of many mystics. In the Christian tradition it often seems that the one element in the human makeup which is to survive the general dissolution of individual qualities is love; and many mystics (although relatively little in the case of Scheffler) expand this love to include not only God but all mankind and, indeed, all creation. Over against the tradition of speculative mysticism, which is concerned with such doctrines as those here described, there is a tradition of emotional mysticism, which, when it does not lose its discipline, is capable of great lyric flight.

But there are problems nevertheless. Within a well-defined religious organization and dogma, mysticism lives continually on the edge of heresy; and the vigorous protestations of orthodoxy on the part of nearly all the Christian mystics do not alter this fact. The rigorous mystic tends to be rather uninterested in the Church. Being convinced of the ultimate impossibility of capturing essential reality through conceptual thinking, fine points of dogma mean little to him. He may well show a certain lofty disdain for ritual and even for the sacraments. And if the mystical effort is a struggle carried on within the confines of his own will, what need has he of a priest? This is not to say that mystics tend to be reformers. Quite the contrary, but they are likely to think, along with Isaiah (1:11), "What to me is the multitude of your sacrifices? says the Lord." So long as mysticism is an elitist matter, confined to a lonely brotherhood of exceptional men, it need not be a threat; but when it becomes a public affair, as it often did in the high and late Middle Ages, the relationship between mysticism and orthodoxy can become touchy indeed. Furthermore, although much mystical writing appears as a commentary upon the Bible, it is difficult to reconcile mystical doctrine with the account of creation given in Genesis, where the world is created *ex nihilo* and is distinctly other than God. The doctrine of emanation tends to make the outlines of God Himself rather diffuse and moves in the direction of a kind of pantheism. Meister Eckhart urges over and over again in his sermons that the experience of the presence of God is available in the smallest object of creation. This is less of a problem in the seventeenth century, with its grim awareness of the transitoriness and meaninglessness of all material things. But another difficulty troubles us when reading Scheffler: the mystical effort seems to wish to make the divine act of creation retroactive, as though it were some sort of mistake. The universe created by God's hand receives a pejorative judgment, and the dominion over the earth which God assigned to man (Gen. 1:26) is distinctly repudiated by the mystic. In fact, creation seems to be nothing but an unfathomable game, sufficient unto itself and without meaning. Böhme, at one point, sees this "spiritual game" esthetically as "a great harmony of many kinds of lute-music, which is all arranged in one single harmony," [6] whereas Scheffler accepts it as the naked will of God:

> *GOtt spielt mit dem Geschöpffe.*
> Diß alles ist ein Spiel/ das Ihr die GOttheit macht:
> Sie hat die Creatur umb Ihret willn erdacht (II, 198).[7]
> (*God Plays with His Creature.*
> All this is a game which the Godhead plays;
> It has thought up the creatures for its own sake.)

Jakob Böhme, indeed, explicitly turned against the Mosaic account of creation.[8] Finally, the language of mysticism, with its hyperboles, its shock effects, and its oblique attacks on normative concepts, is destructive to dogma and frightening to smaller-souled men.

The German tradition, of which Scheffler is a late representative, began to crystallize in the latter part of the thirteenth century. The atmosphere of this period was far removed from the harmonious, well-ordered society which the Romantics attributed to their mythical Middle Ages. It was, in fact, an age of chaos and of extreme anxiety. The Holy Roman Empire lay in ruins: for twenty-three frightening years, from 1250 to 1273, there was not even an emperor. Trust in the secular authority having been shattered, the Church was then shaken by the long schism from 1309 to 1377. As economic relationships began to shift, the towns became embroiled with the princes, the workers with the burghers, and both towns and principalities with Rome. As a result of the many bans and interdicts that flew back and forth, whole communities found themselves barred from the sacraments which were believed to be absolutely essential to salvation. It is no wonder that people began to assemble to search out new forms of religious experience or that women in large numbers fled into the cloisters and religious associations. The Dominicans were assigned the ministry to these orders; and from among them came the mystic Meister Eckhart (*ca.* 1260–1327), by all accounts surely one of the most gifted preachers in Christian history. Widely learned and intensely intellectual, Eckhart pulled the strands of the mystical tradition together into a doctrine which was to live on for centuries in various forms and transmissions. For Eckhart, there is in the soul a *fünkelin,* a little spark, which is of the same essence as the Godhead; and it is by an expansion of this inner divinity at the expense of the individual personality that the transcendence of God can be overcome and man can be *vergotet,* that is, become of the same essence with God. Indeed, since Eckhart appears to differentiate between God and Godhead, which corresponds to the Neoplatonic subordination of the Divine Mind to the comprehensive One, he boldly and hyperbolically intimates that man can reach *beyond* God. This is only part of Eckhart's doctrine, which is complex and subtle; but probably the most significant feature of it is that, by urging men not to attempt to storm Heaven by force, it is aimed against the religious anxieties of the age. At a time when men were tensely worried about the correct way to achieve salvation, and the orders and movements, all in possession of various absolute truths, fought each other bitterly, Eckhart preached *gelâzenheit,* a calm resignation that desires nothing, not even salvation, not even God, an emptying out of the person to allow God to enter it and do His will there without interference. To modern man, with his emphasis upon the development of the individual personality, such a doctrine may mean little, but in the context of Eckhart's time it was a powerful source of consolation. It is worth pointing out that this key aspect of Eckhart's doctrine was clearly missing in the spiritual makeup of Johann Scheffler, despite his acknowledgment of it:

> *GOtt schaut man mit gelassenheit.*
> Der Engel schauet GOtt mit heitern Augen an/
> Ich aber noch vil mehr/ so ich GOtt lassen kan (I, 164).
> *(One Looks at God with Resignation.*
> The angel looks upon God with cheerful eyes,
> But I still more, if I can abandon God.)

Scheffler's later career proves that he was obsessed, in direct contradiction to Eckhart, with finding the clearly defined, authoritative path to salvation; thus he eventually left the mystical way.

Eckhart's strong language and self-possessed character got him into difficulties with Church authority, though he vigorously protested his orthodoxy. When, however, the choleric Pope John XXII finally condemned a number of his doctrines in 1329, Eckhart was dead and could no longer defend himself, so that his name rather fell into oblivion. But his teachings lived on, in somewhat milder form, in the highly popular writings of his pupils Johannes Tauler (*ca.* 1300–1361) and Heinrich Suso (*ca.* 1295–1366; the frequently encountered form "Seuse" is an illegitimate modernization of the original "Siuse"). Tauler is the practical mystic who suited his doctrine to the limitations of his listeners. In his immensely popular sermons, he urges the spiritualization of the affairs of ordinary life. Suso, who according to his autobiography,[9] lived forty years in the harshest asceticism and mortification of the flesh and then gave it up by divine command, applied his lyrical skill to an amalgamation of Eckhart's ideas with the *Frauenmystik* of Mechthild von Magdeburg (*ca.* 1207–83) filled with yearning love for the mystical union.

Following the three great "masters," Eckhart, Tauler, and Suso, the tradition continues, carrying with it the basic elements but constantly varying them and shifting the stresses. The quietistic element of passive and patient waiting for God's call in the soul, which can, but need not necessarily be, derived from Eckhart's doctrine, came to the forefront in the widespread movement of the *Devotio moderna* stemming from the teachings of the Augustinian monk Jan van Ruysbroeck (1293–1381). The anonymous *Theologia Deutsch* (before 1400), which made a strong impression on young Luther, deals seriously with the problem of the will, arguing that the abandonment of the will leads to the experience of Paradise on earth. In another strain, there is a new attention to the phenomena of nature; and the difficult mysticism of the self-taught shoemaker Jakob Böhme (1575–1624) operates largely with symbols of light and darkness taken from the world of nature. The relationship between the enormously influential Böhme and Scheffler is not very clear, although it has been much discussed. Scheffler once asserted, probably somewhat disingenuously, that his reading of Böhme had been one of the experiences that had convinced him of the truth of Catholicism.[10] In fact, however, it would seem logical that congruences of passages of Böhme and Scheffler are on the whole reflections of their common tradition, mainly for two reasons: Böhme's mysticism, though prepared by his reading in the traditional texts, arises primarily out of a series of personal ecstatic experiences of a kind Scheffler seems never to have undergone; and secondly, Böhme's basic posture is theosophical, that is, he proceeds from a mysticism of the heart to a mysticism of the mind, whereas Scheffler's is chiefly intellectual and, indeed, literary.

In general it is not easy to locate Scheffler exactly in the tradition, partly because the basic ideas of the mystics are so much alike, and partly because there is reason to think that Scheffler, in his preface to the *Cherubinic Wanderer,* was at pains to leave out any influence tinged with heresy. Moreover, much of the work done on this problem has been an ax-grinding debate between those who would harness Scheffler to a largely nonexistent special tradition of "German mysticism" and consequently claim him as a pantheist, and those who attempt to defend his Roman Catholic orthodoxy. This is a theological quarrel, however, and Scheffler was not much of a theologian, as his later writings were to show. Furthermore, it is generally agreed that there is little that is original in the mystical content of his epigrams, which reflect rather the common property of the tradition. That he was widely read there can be little doubt. In the preface to the *Cherubinic Wanderer* he refers to Tauler, Ruysbroeck, St. Bernard, St. Bonaventure, and the *Theologia Deutsch,* along with a number of lesser writers. He is also eager to defend himself against an interpretation "that the human soul should or could lose its nature, and be changed by the *Vergöttung* into God or his uncreated essence, which cannot be in all eternity," [11] and he attempts, rather awkwardly, to argue that the soul becomes similar to God through God's grace. This argument, and much of the remainder of the preface, have more to do with Scheffler's concern about his orthodoxy than with the actual content of the *Cherubinic Wanderer;* grace is not a prominent feature of the mystical system reflected in the work. It is rather certain, however, that Scheffler depended heavily on one Catholic source: the *Pro theologia mystica clavis elucidarium* (1640) by the Jesuit Maximilian Sandaeus, a kind of encyclopedia of mystical ideas and their interpretation. Scheffler's copy of this book was extensively annotated, and it seems to have been for him, as the title promises, a key to his mystical studies.[12] It is of considerable significance that Scheffler relied heavily on a compendium rather than on original sources for his studies.

It is difficult to extract a cohesive doctrine from the unsystematically scattered verses of the *Cherubinic Wanderer*. Clearly the overwhelming desideratum is the unity of God's essence with the soul of man. Material creation, human existence, and the human will stand in the way of this unity and must be overcome. What is particularly important for Scheffler's view is that all these things exist in time, whereas the transcendental unity belongs to timeless eternity, the paradisiacal state. Scheffler's verses urge that access to eternity is available to man in the midst of time. In order to find it, man must divest himself of his earthly attributes and discover within himself the *nihil,* the nothingness, which is true divine reality. This is not the *nihil* out of which the world was created in the sense of Genesis, but rather the naught of the Eckhartian tradition, the negative theology of a God without attributes, a reality totally divested of any particularity. This imperative of unity binds God as well as man and is the *sine qua non* of the existence of both. Man may even exceed (the concept of) God as he flows into a transcendental realm beyond both God and man. As for Christ, his Passion is not a historically bound event but one which is repeated continually in every soul, an idea also ultimately traceable to Eckhart. Whereas the human being seems to occupy a special place in the universe as the reconciler of God and His estranged creation, it is also true, as one scholar puts it, that "the colorful rich life which our senses show us is obviously nothing but a heavy, confused dream, out of which to awaken, to sink once again into the dark quiet of the Godhead, should be the most profound desire of our heart." [13] Thus man is exalted as a spiritual being, but as a material being he is less than nothing. God exists in his creatures, but not fully. "Where God and man overlap, facing each other, there is communication; but at the same time, while physically overlapping, they may spiritually turn away from each other, standing back to back, and become reticent." [14] Or, as Scheffler expresses it:

> *GOtt ist allem gleich nahe.*
> GOtt ist dem Belzebub nah wie dem Seraphim:
> Es kehrt nur Belzebub den Rücken gegen jhm (V, 72).
> (*God Is Equally Near to All.*
> God is as near to Beelzebub as to the Seraphim,
> Except that Beelzebub turns his back to him.)

Although more could be said about the doctrine which can be distilled from the *Cherubinic Wanderer* (and there is an extensive literature on the subject), the importance of the work lies not only in the teachings it expresses but also in its poetic achievement, in the compression of ideas into a remarkable form. To appreciate this aspect, we must take a look at the development of Scheffler's form and the use he made of it.

III   *The Formal Tradition*

The Alexandrine line is derived from the Old French *Roman d'Alexandre* and came into German literature by way of sixteenth-century French Renaissance Classicism. It is the most characteristic line form in German Baroque poetry. It consists of six iambic feet with a strong caesura regularly after the third foot. The last foot may have an additional unstressed syllable at the end, giving thirteen rather than twelve syllables. Except when they occur in sonnets, Alexandrines are usually rhymed in pairs. The steady beat of the Alexandrine can be rather monontonous, and for this reason some seventeenth-century German poetry becomes wearisome over long stretches. It does, however, have considerable expressive possibilities; and in the hands of a master like Andreas Gryphius, whose heavy style often strains even such a long line to an agonizing degree, the effect can be moving indeed. Furthermore, the strong break in the middle of the line encourages an intellectualized, antithetical kind of poetic expression, which is well suited to the dualism and tensions so prominent in the thinking and apperception of German authors at this time. Put together in a couplet, the four half-lines form a chiastic arrangement with a variety of epigrammatic possibilities. Martin Opitz, with his well-developed sense for what could be done in German poetry with the means he knew, wrote epigrams, as did Gryphius; and among the finest minor works of the age are the epigrams of Friedrich von Logau (1605–55), a witty and sardonic Silesian who seems to have been transplanted from the eighteenth into the seventeenth century. The religious epigram has a Latin tradition behind it. Because of certain echoes, it seems possible that Scheffler knew a work by Johann Theodor von Tschesch (1595–1649), *Vitae cum Christo sive Epigrammatum sacrorum Centuriae XII*, published in 1644.[15] Abraham von Franckenberg also wrote epigrams, and it is out of his circle that the clearest formal influence upon the *Cherubinic Wanderer* comes.

Daniel Czepko von Reigersfeld (1605–60) was a man of unusually wide interests. At various times in his active life he was a lawyer, physician, farmer, historian, public official, and politician, as well as a writer. His intellectual interests were equally extensive. Like Scheffler, he had been influenced by the Humanist Christoph Köler, and he was learned particularly in foreign languages, art, and religion. Through several Silesian noblemen, including Franckenberg, Czepko had connections with the Böhme circle, and it seems that it is by this route that the mystical strain entered into his writings. It is rather doubtful whether Czepko is to be classified as a mystic as such, in the sense of one who has had a mystical experience which is central to his spiritual life. Rather, like Franckenberg, and perhaps also Scheffler, whose actual felt mystical experience is doubtful, Czepko combined what he had learned of the mystical tradition with a not inconsiderable talent for writing. Czepko's central religious concern appears to have been not mystical union but death. In the midst of his busy life in the secular world he was prey to anxieties about death which he allayed by a variety of religious speculations; many of his works were written in a spirit of consolation on the occasion of someone's death.[16]

The extant manuscript of Czepko's *Sexcenta monodisticha sapientium* begins with a dedication to Duke Wilhelm of Saxe-Weimar, the third president of the highly influential literary association called the Fruchtbringende Gesellschaft, and is dated 1655.[17] From Czepko's own account in the introduction, however, it is clear that the work was completed around 1648. Why Czepko did not publish the work for which he is best remembered is not known (it was not printed in full until our own century), but it seems to have circulated widely in manuscript. Since it is generally assumed that Scheffler must have written much of the *Cheru-*

binic Wanderer before his conversion in 1653 and that he became acquainted with Czepko's work through Franckenberg, who died the year before, it is thought that Scheffler saw the work sometime between 1650, when Franckenberg returned to Silesia, and 1652. But whether it was then or somewhat later, there can be little doubt that Czepko's *Monodisticha* were a major inspiration for the *Cherubinic Wanderer.*

Unlike Scheffler, Czepko restricts himself exclusively to couplets and, also unlike him, they are evenly divided into six books of one hundred couplets apiece. Each book, in addition, has an introductory sonnet. As in the *Cherubinic Wanderer,* there is no discernible thematic order to the succession of verses. Some of the verbal echoes are so compelling that it is possible to believe that Scheffler had the work, or excerpts from it, before him when he was composing his own verses. For example:

Czepko:
> *Auff mit dem Hertzen!*
> Verächtlich ist der Mensch, der untern Menschen lebt
> Und sich nicht über das, was menschlich ist, erhebt (I, 46).
> (*Up with the Heart!*
> Contemptible is the man who lives among men
> And does not lift himself beyond that which is human.)

Scheffler:
> *Erheb dich über dich.*
> Der Mensch der seinen Geist nicht über sich erhebt/
> Der ist nicht wehrt daß er im Menschenstande lebt (II, 22).
> (*Lift Yourself Above Yourself.*
> The man who does not lift his spirit above itself
> He is not worthy of living in the human condition.)

Czepko:
> *Kein Wesen ohne Gott.*
> Indem der Teuffel ist, ist er so gut als du,
> Dem Wesen nach, in Gott, nichts mangelt ihm, als Ruh (IV, 5).
> (*No Being Without God.*
> The Devil, by being, is as good as you;
> In his essence, in God, he lacks nothing but peace.)

Scheffler:
> *Der Teuffel der ist gut.*
> Der Teuffel ist so gutt dem Wesen nach als du.

Waß gehet ihm dann ab? Gestorbner will' und ruh (V, 30).
  (*The Devil Is Good.*
The Devil is as good as thou if Being is the test.
What is that the Devil lacks? Peace and a Will at rest.)
                                        [Flitch, p. 169.] [18]

In these two examples, chosen from among a number of possible ones, the diction is so close, not to mention the identical rhymes, that it is unreasonable to doubt the connection. Apart from these close verbal correspondences, there are also many verses in the *Cherubinic Wanderer* that are similar to Czepko's in content, e.g.:

Czepko:
  Nichts in der Zeit, als den Leib.
Der Weise, wo er steht, weiß nichts von Ort und Zeit:
Er lebt zwar hier, und ist doch in der Ewigkeit (III, 13).
    (*Nothing in Time but the Body.*
The wise man, wherever he stands, knows nothing of place and time;
He lives here, to be sure, is yet in eternity.)

Scheffler:
  Man muß sich überschwenken.
Mensch, wo du deinen Geist schwingst über Ort uñ Zeit/
So kanstu jeden blik seyn in der Ewigkeit (I, 12).
    (*One Must Surpass Himself.*
Man, when you raise your spirit beyond time and place,
You can every moment be in eternity.)

Such examples could be supplied in considerable numbers.

At this point the question of Scheffler's originality arises, since it has been established that the mystical content of his verses is the common coin of the tradition to which he had access and that its formal expression is so obviously influenced by Czepko's work. Certainly the verses of the *Monodisticha* were no mean achievement. In style and purity of language Czepko belongs to the school of Martin Opitz. Although he remained through his life an orthodox Lutheran, and his epigrams lack the last measure of daring which is possible in mystical poetry, he not infrequently produces a startling effect. An example of Czepko at his best is the following epigram:

[50]

> *Ein besser als Aus.*
> Ich gieng in Gott, und nichts sprach allda: Wer bist du?
> Ich floß aus Gott, und schau, es sprach drauff alles: Ruh (IV, 58).
>   (*In Better than Out.*
> I went into God, nothing said Who goes there?
> I flowed out of God, and look, everything then spoke peace.)

The unspoken intimations of this couplet are effective despite the butchered rhythm in the first line. But this is Czepko's weakness: despite his insight into the possibilities of the Alexandrine couplet for antithetical and paradoxical statement, he did not really master the form. His rhythms are rough and often do not fit well into the metrical pattern. He lacks ease of syntax, one of the last skills mastered in the stylistic renewal of the German Baroque, so that the sentences of which his couplets are formed can be awkward to the point of incomprehensibility. It was this mastery of the form, as well as a more startling juxtaposition of concepts, which Scheffler achieved; and it is for this reason, and not for his originality and inventiveness, that Scheffler is remembered beyond Czekpo and the other epigrammists of the century. A further example illustrates this difference.

Czepko:
> *Gott siehet Niemand als Gott.*
> Wer Gott wil sehn, der muß in Gottes Wesen steigen:
> Denn Gott wil sich bloß Gott sonst keinem Dinge zeigen (VI, 3).
>   (*God Sees No One but God.*
> Whoever wants to see God must ascend into God's being,
> For God wants to show himself only to God and to no other thing.)

Scheffler:
> *Der geistliche Berg.*
> Ich bin ein Berg in GOtt/ und muß mich selber steigen/
> Daferne GOtt mir sol sein liebes Antlitz zeigen (II, 83).
>   (*The Spiritual Mountain.*
> I am a hill of God, and must myself ascend
> That God may then reveal his face to me, my friend.)
>   [Bilger, p. 5.] [19]

Working with the same rhymes and a related idea, Scheffler enriches Czepko's statement with the metaphor of the mountain, which then releases the verb *steigen* ("ascend") and further allows an image of a kind characteristic of Scheffler, that of the mystic ascending himself, that is to say, climbing beyond himself, to reach the sight of God. Furthermore, the rhythmic curve is much improved. Czepko's second line is made awkward by the dative appositive, where Scheffler, again characteristically, forms a simple free-flowing clause strung neatly between subordinating conjunction and final verb, making effective use of this feature of German syntax.

There are few poets in German literature who have succeeded in extracting so many possibilities from a single limited form as Scheffler did from the Alexandrine couplet. It is not unjust to think of Heine's folk-song stanza and his "Spanish" trochees, or Rilke's variations on the sonnet. On the whole, Scheffler adheres strictly to the rules established for the Alexandrine by Opitz, especially those to the effect that there must be no internal rhyme with the word appearing in the third foot before the caesura, and that the lines are end-stopped.[20] Within this strict pattern, however, a nearly inexhaustible wealth of possibilities is spread before the reader of the *Cherubinic Wanderer,* only a few aspects of which can be touched upon here.[21] The Alexandrine couplet is not a lyrical form—Scheffler demonstrated his lyrical talents in his other major work, the *Holy Joy of the Soul*—but a dialectical spoken verse with an intellectual, though often irrational, content. Two major types of statement recur consistently in the *Cherubinic Wanderer,* one of which can be called, in general terms, the logical reversal of a relation, and the other a statement of negation, i.e., $A \neq A, A = B$. An example of the first is the following:

> *GOtt schauet man an sich.*
> Wie ist mein GOtt gestalt? Geh schau dich selber an/
> Wer sich in GOtt beschaut/ schaut Gott warhafftig an (II, 157).
> (*One Sees God in Himself.*
> How is God formed? Go, take a look at yourself,
> Whoever sees himself in God, truly looks at God.)

Here the logical relation that is forced upon the mind by our usage of language—the otherness of God—is reversed from the mystical perspective by urging the presence of the self in God. There are a number of possibilities. For example, there can be a parallel reversal of the metaphors in a line:

> *Der Mensch ist eine Kohle.*
> Mensch du bist eine Kohl/ GOtt ist dein Feur uñ Licht:
> Du bist schwarz/ finster/ kalt/ liegstu in Ihme nicht (IV, 133).
> (*Man Is a Coal.*
> Man, thou art but a coal; God is thy fire and light.
> Thou art black, dull and cold, unsheltered by his might.
> [Bilger, p. 109.]

Another possiblity is the antithetical juxtaposition of various modes and actions:

> [*Die Gelassenheit.*]
> Geh auß/ so geht Gott ein: Stirb dir/ so lebstu GOtt:
> Sey nicht/ so ist es Er: thu nichts/ so gschicht's Geboth (II, 136).
> (*Abandonment.*
> Go out—and so God goeth in; die to thyself—thou hast begun
> To live to God; Be not—He is—Do naught—His bidding's done.)
> [Flitch, p. 145.]

It is natural that statements of negation should play a large part in the *Cherubinic Wanderer* because of the importance of "negative theology" [22] for the mystical tradition. It is a way of coping with the fact that the subjects of mystical speculation are ineffable and can be intimated only by saying what they are not. A rational idea can be turned into its opposite by an unexpected denial:

> *GOtt betrübt die Sünde nicht.*
> GOtt thut die Sünde weh in dir als seinem Sohn:
> In seiner GOttheit selbst/ da fühlt Er nichts davon (V, 328).
> (*Sin Troubleth Not God.*
> God feeleth pain for sin in thee as in His son
> But in His self of Deity He feeleth none.)
> [Flitch, p. 104.]

The negation can be a more indirect one between two opposed spheres of being:

Der mensch ist zwey Menschen.
Zwey Menschen sind in mir: Der eine wil was GOtt:
Der andre was die Welt der Teuffel und der Tod (V, 120).
   (*A Man Is Two Men.*
There are two men in me; one wants the will of God,
The other the will of the world, the devil, and of death.)

   An important characteristic of the Alexandrine line is the caesura, which normally falls after the third foot. This break in the
line, depending on how strong the stress is on the syllable preceding, can be of greater or lesser strength, giving four basic possibilities of division for the couplet. If both caesuras are strong, the
couplet can be divided into four equal parts, a pattern Scheffler
often uses for metaphorical equations:

   Das geheime Königreich.
Ich bin ein Königreich/ mein Hertz das ist der Thron/
Die Seel ist Königin/ der König GOttes Sohn (III, 131).
   (*The Secret Kingdom.*
I am a kingdom, my heart it is the throne,
The soul is the queen, the king is God's own son.)

The same division can yield three items plus a summation, as illustrated by one of Scheffler's occasional uses of alchemical metaphor:

   Die Tingierung.
Der heilge Geist der schmeltzt/ der Vater der verzehrt/
Der Sohn ist die Tinctur, die Gold macht und verklärt (I, 246).
   (*The Transmutation.*
The Holy Ghost which melts, the Father who consumes,
The Son is the tincture, which makes and transfigures gold.)

If both caesuras are weak and hardly felt, the couplet acquires a
more lyrical quality and can also establish a dialectic between two
full lines:

   Die Bach wird das Meer.
Hier flüss' ich noch in GOtt als eine Bach der Zeit;
Dort bin ich selbst das Meer der ewgen Seeligkeit (IV, 135).

   [54]

>(*Brooks Becomes Seas.*
>Here I still flow in God as a small stream of time,
>There I shall be a sea of blessedness sublime.)
>   [Bilger, p. 15.]

In the two full lines a combination of main clause and subordinate clause often establishes the dialectic. If-then structures are not infrequent:

>*Unvollkommene gestorbenheit.*
>Wo dich noch diß und das bekümmert und bewegt/
>So bistu noch nicht gantz mit GOtt ins Grab gelegt (I, 134).
>(*Not Perfectly Dead.*
>If over this and that thou makest such a stir,
>Then art thou not yet laid with God in the sepulchre.)
>   [Flitch, p. 124.]

The third possibility, a sharp caesura in the first line and a weak one in the second, is what Elisabeth Spörri calls "the mystical epigram par excellence" [23] because the break in the first line brings a sharp antithesis which, in the second, is resolved to a mystical paradox:

>*Die Ruh und Würkung GOttes.*
>GOtt hat sich nie bemüht/ auch nie geruht/ das merk:
>Sein Wirken ist sein ruhn/ und seine Ruh sein Werk (IV, 166).
>(*The Rest and Work of God.*
>Rested God never has, nor toiled—'tis manifest,
>For all His rest is work and all His work is rest.)
>   [Flitch, p. 103.]

This pattern encourages the very characteristic occurrence of a striking statement in the first half-line, followed by a sharp caesura and then an exegesis of the statement:

>*Wer wil wird GOtt gebohrn.*
>Von GOtt wird GOtt gebohrn: sol er dich den gebehrn/
>So mustu jhm zuvor den Willn darzu gewehrn (VI, 129).
>(*Whoever Will, Is Born God.*
>God is born from God; if he is to give birth to you,
>Then you must first grant him the will for it.)

The fourth possibility of a weak caesura in the first line and a sharp one in the second is not quite as important for the *Cherubinic Wanderer,* but there are a number of interesting instances where the break in rhythm appears elsewhere in the line. This can be an effective variation because the proper place for the caesura is felt by the reader of the Alexandrine to be after the third foot. The contrast between a "regular" first line and an "irregular" second one can effectively suggest the confusion of the wrongly located soul:

> *In der Sonnen ists gut seyn.*
> Wer in der Sonnen ist/ dem mangelt nicht das Licht/
> Das dem/ der ausser jhr verjrret geht/ gebricht (I, 112).
> (*It Is Good to Be in the Sun.*
> Whoever is in the sun does not lack the light
> Which he who wanders out of it must do without.)

There also may be multiple breaks in the rhythmic line caused by the piling up of monosyllables in series, particularly of nouns, a stylistic feature which Scheffler shares with many other poets of his time. Occasionally there occurs a particularly sharp cut after the first foot of the first line, which has the effect of placing a heavy stress on the word which precedes it:

> *Die Verklärung.*
> Mein Leib der wird für GOtt wie ein Carfunkel stehn/
> Wenn seine grobheit wird im Feuer untergehn (II, 110).
> (*The Transfiguration.*
> My body will stand before God like a garnet,
> When its crudeness perishes in the fire.)

The foregoing are just a few examples of the range of Scheffler's use of form in the *Cherubinic Wanderer.* There is not space here to do any justice to other important topics, such as the varieties of rhythmic curve, or the quality of Scheffler's sound and rhymes. Particularly, his metaphorical usage needs more study than it has yet received. Furthermore, it should not be forgotten that Sheffler's artistic mastery was undoubtedly a gift of genius, for there can be little doubt that he did not regard his work as literature in the modern sense, as a creative achievement sufficient unto itself, but rather as writing with a purpose. The form is a tool to lever the reader out of the complacency of his stock responses and make him see the words and concepts of the epigram in a new light, so as to intensify his religious sensibilities and carry him beyond earth-bound logic. The method is one of surprise: the astonishing statement, the alogical phrase, the continual application of the irrational and the contradictory. Scheffler does not stratify the world he grasps, or differentiate between higher and lower orders of that which is perceivable. Therefore he can say nearly anything he pleases, so long as it arouses the reader to a comprehension or even a suspicion of the higher, ineffable state toward which the mystic proceeds. It is a kind of purpose which encourages self-contradiction and even the abuse of words. It is true, to be sure, that not all, or perhaps not even the majority, of the couplets have this effect, for many are indistinguishable from simple religious homiletics; and there are noticeably uninspired stretches in the third and fourth books and particularly in Book VI. But the force of his best epigrams derives from the unusual, if not completely original, treatment he gives to matters of common concern to all men. It will therefore be appropriate to select a few of the topics which are prominent in the *Cherubinic Wanderer* and to examine the various ways in which Scheffler deals with them.

IV *God*

For the Christian mystic the overriding purpose in life is to achieve union with God. Scheffler's rhetoric, his browbeating, and his exhortation struggle to lead, drive, or even frighten the reader into this achievement. The way seems to pass beyond the Kingdom of Heaven, despite those verses (especially in the sixth book) that make use of the traditional mythology of the Heavenly population. The mystic would have Bunyan's pilgrim travel one step farther, coming to the end of his journey not at the foot of God's throne, but as an integral part of His being. Of necessity, then, the communicating mystic is forced to say something about the nature of God.

The word "forced" is properly applied here, for Scheffler's statements about God have a slightly embarrassed undertone. Here, as nowhere else, the innate ineffability of mystical perceptions raises problems and paradoxes. The poet is plagued by the knowledge that whatever he might say about God will be incomplete, insufficient, and distortive. He hesitates, therefore, to make any statement that will make it appear as though he is creating God in his own image. To make his assertion he is forced to every kind of circumlocution, antithetical device, and overwhelming statement of which his poetic talent is capable.

One of the most important aspects of Christian mysticism is its separation of the active *deity* from *divinity*, the only characteristic of the latter being existence. One scholar explains it in this way:

Scholasticism was accustomed . . . to differentiate *Divinitas* from *Deus,* the essence of God from its actuation into the Trinity of three persons. This differentiation, which had only a logical basis, not an objective one, is reiterated in Eckhart's *gotheit* and *got.* Godhead is for him the absolute being completely without characteristics, toward which the soul directs its ultimate efforts. "God has an effect, Godhead has no effect, it has nothing to effect, no works take place in it. It has never intended any works. The difference between God and Godhead lies in effect and non-effect." [24]

This distinction is extremely important and will become even more so when we view the relationship between God and man. It is only this distinction that permits Scheffler to speak of God at all or to make some of his startling statements about Him. This is not to say that he makes the distinction consistently, which is certainly not the case. But a tacit understanding that even God is but an emanation from an ideal divinity superior to Him must lie behind some of his epigrams.

Nevertheless, the God who is distinguished from the essence of divinity in this way still lies, by and large, beyond the power of our conception. The late medieval author of the *Theologia Deutsch* phrases the matter with his characteristic simplicity and neatness: "Look, now were God something, this or that, then He would not be all things and above all things as He is, and thus He would also not be truly perfect. Therefore: God is, and yet is neither this nor that, which a creature, as creature, could know, name, think, or speak." [25] The distinction, then, is not as clear or helpful as might first appear. But one important characteristic is predicated here: Perfection. Completeness, perfection, are what God is; and this characteristic is closely connected with the total oneness of the universe which mysticism maintains.[26]

The importance of the name of God is an element out of the Old Testament. To name a thing is not only to identify it but to delimit it. The name assumes an existence in and of itself. To name God is therefore an impertinence, for if He has a name, it is unspeakable. The same kind of idea reappears in the concept of the Word. Throughout the Old Testament the Word of God is an active force in its own right, which has the power to accomplish that which it expresses. In the Christian tradition, God becomes the Word in the famous opening verse of John that caused Goethe's Faust so much difficulty. The Word, the *logos,* is one of the elements of the Divine Trinity.

The concept of the Trinity is more prominent in Scheffler's thought than is usual in the mystical tradition. He does not probe the concept of three persons in one God to its depths, but still he calls upon it as a tool of expression:

> *Der Punct/ die Linie und Fläche.*
> GOtt Vatter ist der Punct; auß Ihm fleust GOtt der Sohn
> Die Linie: GOtt der Geist ist beider Fläch' und Kron (IV, 62).
> (*The Point, the Line, and Surface.*
> God Father is a point, God Son the circuit line,
> And God the Ghost does both as area combine.)
> [Carus, p. 21.] [27]

Although Scheffler draws this sort of thing from Christian tradition, it will be noted that he discusses the Trinity in terms of simile and metaphor (cf. also I, 148), so that doctrinal precision is avoided.

With these points in mind, we may now turn to the way in which Scheffler introduces God to his reader, so to speak. In doing so, we cannot begin to exhaust the wealth of his epigrams on the subject. We shall select just a few to illustrate his approach. Scheffler seeks primarily to erase any presuppositions about the nature of God which his reader may bring with him. A verse of extreme negation appears, therefore, very close to the beginning of the work:

GOtt ergreifft man nicht.
GOtt ist ein lauter nichts/ Ihn rührt kein Nun noch Hier:
Je mehr du nach Ihm greiffst/ je mehr entwird Er dir (I, 25).
　(*One Does Not Grasp God.*
No here nor now can touch God, who is nothingness;
The more we reach for him, the more he vanishes.)
[Trask, p. 16.] [28]

In this often quoted verse the basic premise is clearly spelled out. It is both a statement and a warning. One cannot grasp God: He is nothingness. In reaching for Him one drives Him away. The blunt statement of this point reduces all speculation upon the nature of God to naught. The statement can be more radical:

Auch von GOtt.
GOtt ist noch nie gewest/ und wird auch niemals seyn/
Und bleibt doch nach der Welt/ war auch vor jhr allein
　(III, 181).
　(*Also about God.*
God never did exist, nor ever will, yet aye
He was ere worlds began, and when they're gone He'll stay.)
[Carus, p. 20.]

Behind this verse one almost hears the Zen monk striving to jolt his disciple to enlightenment by saying, "There is no Buddha." The paradox, as it is presented here, hardly allows a rational resolution in normal language. However, it is clear that there is no denial here of God's existence per se, but that Scheffler is denying the possibility of predicating past and future to that existence. Even with this, the rational content of the epigram is not solved. It depends far more on its effect than on its logical content.

Scheffler makes use of one of his longer verses to stress this aspect of negative theology:

Der unerkandte GOtt.
Was GOtt ist weiß man nicht: Er ist nicht Licht/ nicht Geist/
Nicht Wonnigkeit/ nicht Eins/ nicht was man Gottheit heist:
Nicht Weißheit/ nicht Verstand/ nicht Liebe/ Wille/ Gütte:
Kein Ding/ kein Unding auch/ kein Wesen/ kein Gemütte:

> Er ist was ich/ und du/ und keine Creatur/
> Eh wir geworden sind was Er ist/ nie erfuhr (IV, 21).
> > (*The Unknown God.*
> What God is one knows not: He is not light, not spirit,
> Not joy, not unity, not what one calls Godhead:
> Not wisdom, not sense, not love, will, goodness:
> No thing, no non-thing either, no being, no mind:
> He is what I, and you, and any creature,
> Never learned before we have become what He is.)

Here every conceivable quality that one might normally predicate to God, even the Johannine quality of light, so important for the mystic, is denied as insufficient, in a choppy verse which seems to tear at the fabric of its own language. God is beyond our poor power to conceive, yet He is open to us nonetheless if we can achieve union.

These statements are basic to all that follows and modify the other verses on the subject. Whatever Scheffler may say about God otherwise is subordinate to the acknowledgment of ineffability here expressed, and thus is not descriptive, but strives for an effect upon the reader's mode of thinking. Other verses, however, do attempt to open new avenues of approach.

> *GOtt ist das kleinst' und gröste.*
> Mein GOtt wie groß ist GOtt Mein GOtt wie klein ist GOtt!
> Klein als da kleinste ding/ und groß wie alls/ von noth (II, 40).
> > (*God Is the Smallest and the Greatest.*
> My God, how great is God! My God, how God is small!
> Small as the smallest thing, great—needs must be—as All.)
> > > [Flitch, p. 111.]

The couplet is marred by the weak filler which serves as a rhyme in the second line, but it is significant because it represents two typical elements of Scheffler's style. By the use of superlatives he tries to define the boundaries of God in various categories of infinitude: He is at once the greatest and smallest of all things. The second device the poet calls to his aid is that of antithesis: God's being at once the greatest and smallest expresses His fullness, His perfection, His all-inclusiveness and oneness, which is a major foundation of the mystical structure.

>   *GOtt ist Fünsternuß und Licht.*
> GOtt ist ein lautrer Blitz/ und auch ein Tunkles nicht/
> Das keine Creatur beschaut mit jhren Licht (II, 146).
>   (*God Is Darkness and Light.*
> God is a pure lightning, and also a dark nothing,
> That no creature can see with its own light.)

Here the antithesis is brought brilliantly into play. Even though, or just because, God is as bright as the lightning, or dark as nothingness, it is not possible for man to look upon Him or identify Him. For Scheffler's purposes, however, these statements permit of still further modification:

>   *GOtt nichts und alles.*
> GOtt ist ein Geist/ ein Feur/ ein Wesen und ein Licht:
> Und ist doch wiederumb auch dieses alles nicht (IV, 38).
>   *God Is All and Nothing.*
> God is a spirit, a fire, an essence, and a light;
> And is yet on the other hand not all these things either.)

Here Scheffler permits metaphors to be applied to God which are of the most ethereal nature, but then, as though embarrassed by his own impertinence, he immediately denies his own statement. The effect of the contradictory statements is meant to work upon the reader simultaneously, producing a dim apprehension of what God is "something like," although the last word is that of denial.

Whatever God is, He is what He wills Himself to be. He is immediately the result of His will, without any cause-and-effect relationship intervening between the will and the essence:

>   *GOtt ist das was Er wil.*
> GOtt ist ein Wunderding; Er ist das was Er wil/
> Und wil das was Er ist ohn alle maß und Ziehl (I, 40).
>   (*God Is What He Wills.*
> God is a wondrous thing: He wills that which He is
> And is that which He wills, with no end and no cause.)
>   [Trask, p. 18.]

The word *Wunderding*, it seems, is as close as Scheffler cares to come to the idea of a Holy Mystery, that particular area of dogma

which is completely inaccessible to human reason. In a sense, all
reality, all existence, is a mystery to man, who can understand
only his one purpose of uniting himself with God. The relationship will ↔ being is reciprocal and perfect; there is an implicit
comparison here to imperfect man, who is quite often far less than
what he wills. The same thought is more strongly expressed in this
example:

> *GOtt wird was Er wil.*
> GOtt ist ein Ewger Geist/ der alls wird was Er wil/
> Und bleibt doch wie Er ist Unformlich und ohn Ziehl (V, 358).
>   *(God Becomes What He Wills.*
> God is an endless force that what it wills attaineth,
> That formless, without goal, still as it is remaineth.)
>   [Bilger, p. 31.]

Scheffler's insistence on God's lack of purpose, in dramatic contra-
distinction to the popular belief that God has ends in view to
which man must accommodate himself, is another way of driving
home the point that goals imply a process of becoming, whereas
God is perfect, and *is* in his timelessness, and therefore cannot
become or strive after goals. Approaching the matter in another
way, Scheffler, as other mystical writers before him, retreats into a
type of hyperbole which is impermissible in the logic of language
usage and therefore transcends it:

> *Daβ wesen GOttes.*
> Was ist das wesen GOtts? Fragstu mein ängigkeit?
> Doch wisse/ daβ es ist ein' überwesenheit (II, 145).
>   *(The Essence of God.*
> What is the essence of God? Do you ask my narrowness?
> But know that it is an over-essence.)

Here Scheffler underlines his own incompetence to describe the
nature of God and creates a superlative out of a noun which does
not ordinarily receive such a prefix. This use of the superlative
prefix *über-* is again not original with Scheffler but is traditional in
the mystical vocabulary and derives from the Greek prefix ὑπερ-
as used by Pseudo-Dionysius.[29]

It is perhaps only the distinction between God and Godhead,

the subordination of *Deus* to *Divinitas,* that permits Scheffler to make statements which seem as daring as the following:

> *GOtt kan sich selbst nicht messen.*
> GOtt ist so hoch und groß/ wolt' Er sich selber messen/
> Er würd/ ob er gleich Gott/ deß Maßstabs zahl vergessen
>   (V, 280).
>   (*God Cannot Measure Himself.*
> God is so high and great, that if He would measure Himself,
> He would, although God, forget the count of the measure.)

This reminds one of a little of the hoary sophistries of the logical-minded such as: "If God is omnipotent, can He make a rock He cannot break?" Scheffler's alogical rhetoric is completely unperturbed by such considerations. In fact, he turns them to his advantage by using them to cast doubt not on God but on the use of language. When he is insisting upon the greatness of God, he is perfectly willing to shock the reader by baldly asserting that even God is incapable of measuring himself. This is poetry, not theology; Scheffler is confident that he is not diminishing the stature of God in the reader's mind by such a statement but is rather convincing the reader of God's incomprehensible greatness. A similar verse is even rougher in its mode of expression:

> *GOtt weiß jhm keinen Anfang.*
> Du fragst/ wie lange GOtt gewest sey? umb bericht:
> Ach schweig: es ist so lang'/ Er weiß es selber nicht (III, 180).
>   (*God Knoweth Not His Beginning.*
> How long hath God been God? Be silent, ask not this!
> So long, God knoweth not Himself how long it is.)
>   [Flitch, p. 160.]

If there is some slight crudity here, there is no impiety. The contempt expressed by *Ach schweig* is turned against men who persist in speculating upon what in Scheffler's terms is nonsense.

The position of love in Christian mysticism is reputed to be somewhat restricted. The responsibility of man to love his fellow man is said to drop almost completely out of view. An attentive reading of the mystics does not bear this out. Eckhart emphasizes repeatedly that a kindness done is better than a prayer: "If one were in such an ecstasy as St. Paul in his time, and knew a sick man who required a bowl of soup, I regard it as far better that you should leave off ecstasy out of love and serve the needy man in a greater love." [30] Many of his successors continue this attitude. However, what might be called a kind of lateral generosity of heart, a transference of the love of God to his creatures also, who are after all in a mystical sense a part of his being, does seem somewhat lacking in Scheffler's character. For him love belongs to God, and does not appear at first sight to be returned. A series of verses will illustrate this.

> *Der Geist vertrit uns.*
> GOtt liebt und lobt sich selbst/ so viel er immer kan:
> Er kniet und neiget sich/ Er betht sich selber an (I, 236).
> (*The Spirit Represents Us.*
> God loves and lauds himself as much as ever he may;
> He kneels and bends and bows and to himself doth pray.)
> [Trask, p. 32.]

The expression here is strange. The picture of God loving Himself in almost narcissistic fashion is likely make the modern reader uncomfortable, but its further development is most interesting.

> *GOtt muß sich selber lieben.*
> GOtt ist das höchste Gutt/ er muß jhm selbst gefallen/
> Sich selber auf sich kehrn/ sich lieben/ ehrn/ für allen (V, 42).
> (*God Must Love Himself.*
> God is the highest good, He must please Himself,
> Turn to Himself, love and honor Himself before all.)

Here is a case where logic is at work. The nature of God demands love. It follows, therefore, that He must love Himself. Scheffler is not averse to calling upon logic, unbound by it though he may be, when it will serve his purpose of expression. The purpose of these verses is to make men see, and it can be achieved by a sudden access of logic as well as a sharp cut across the intellectual grain. Another couplet carries the implied syllogism a step further:

GOtt liebt nichts als sich.
GOtt hat sich selbst so lieb/ bleibt jhm so zugethan;
Daß er auch nimmermehr was anders lieben kan (V, 34).
   (*God Loveth Naught but Himself.*
God is so dear unto Himself, folded in self so utterly,
That He can never cherish love for anything that is not He.)
[Flitch, p. 104.]

Here is the most radical expression of the idea: God loves nothing outside of Himself. This is by no means a rejection of the possibility that man may receive God's love; rather it looks ahead to the culmination of the whole mystical process (the subject of our next section), for man must become a part of God before he can participate in God's love.

V *God and I*

The *Cherubinic Wanderer* contains no single subject which is probed with greater energy, variety, or concern than that of the relationship between God and man. This is not to be wondered at, since this relationship is central to the thought of Christian mysticism, as it is to much of religion generally. Contemplation of such matters as death, eternity, and the nature of God is really only ancillary to this concern, and serves only to define the universe in which this singularly crucial relationship takes place.

The relationship is not so much one between God and man, taken in the abstract, but between God and the I, an intensely personal bond which is so vital and all-encompassing that the individual's consciousness of the world around him and indeed, to a great extent, of the rest of humanity fades into the background. Scheffler speaks about "I" and "thou," almost never of "we" or "you" in the plural. His insights into the relationship he seeks to achieve with God are personal to an extreme degree; and when he speaks to his readers, as he often does, he speaks to the individual and not to the community. The Christian ideal of an ordered community under God is totally subordinated in the passion of the individual striving for the *unio mystica*.

In this study we can deal with only a few of the verses on this subject. The selection of verses considered here may require some defense, and it will be well to keep in mind what aspect of the matter we are considering. There are two rather large categories of verses which will not be treated. One is the group which uses the mannerisms of *Jesusminne,* the sensual, often erotic elaboration of the idea of the Christian as bride of Jesus, the central theme of the *Holy Joy of the Soul.* This topic is better considered in our chapter on that more "Seraphic" work. The other set is made up of a large number of verses which have a predominantly homiletic or didactic character and which are not essentially different from religious poetry of many other genres. They do not participate in the mystical tradition to any great degree. We shall concentrate on a selection of those epigrams in which the mystical content has been honed to a fine edge and in which this content is presented in imaginative and startling form. As a result, it will be found that our selection reflects to an extent the changing character of the *Cherubinic Wanderer,* with the major emphasis on verses from Books I and II, followed by Book V. Fewer examples are chosen from Books III and IV, and none at all will appear here from the more orthodox and conservative Book VI. Even so, we shall have given only a cursory sampling of the wealth and brilliance of this material in the work. We shall approach the matter from several different standpoints.

(1) *Resignation.* The advantage of an irrational viewpoint is that it enables one to work both sides of a dialectic. The mystical tradition often urges men to strive actively for the desired union with God. Scheffler has such verses (e.g. III, 58, 59, 182; VI, 55, 56, 74, 75), and the title of one of Czepko's couplets (VI, 26) is "You Must Sweat." On the other hand, the tradition places great value upon *Gelassenheit,* the resignation of abandonment of self which permits the union to happen to one. The soul must make room to receive God (cf. Philippians 2:7) through a process of *Absterben der Ichheit* ("dying away of I-ness"), and as soon as one makes an active gesture to take God by storm, He becomes a phantom that will not be grasped. Somehow the individual must empty himself of desire and self-concern before God can find entrance:

> *Du must nichts seyn/ nichts wollen.*
> Mensch/ wo du noch was bist/ was weist/ was liebst und hast;
> So bistu/ glaube mir/ nicht ledig deiner Last (I, 24).

(*Thou Must Be Nothing, Want Nothing.*
Man, if thou still be aught, aught know, aught love or hate,
Believe me, thou hast not cast off thy burden's weight.)
[Trask, p. 16.]

This extreme form of self-abandonment is of course a major feature of Oriental religion; and it is here that one of the noticeable similarities between Eastern and Western mysticism is to be found. In this couplet it comes clearly to the fore. As long as one knows something, loves, hates or even is, the way to God is not open. The connection is clarified in the following epigram:

Nichts wollen macht Gotte gleich.
GOtt ist die Ewge Ruh/ weil Er nichts sucht noch wil:
Wiltu ingleichen nichts/ so bistu eben vil (I, 76).
(*To Will Naught Is to Be Like God.*
Willing and seeking naught, God is eternal peace:
Willest thou likewise naught, thy peace is even as His.)
[Flitch, p. 119.]

Somehow the individual must put himself in harmony with the immovable calm of God in order to participate in God's being. Scheffler hammers at this idea again and again, trying to break the chains of earth-bound man.

The key word for this state of being appears in a title:

Die Gelassenheit.
So vil du Gott geläst/ so vil mag Er dir werden,
Nicht minder und nicht mehr hilfft Er dir auß beschwerden
(I, 22).
(*Abandonment.*
As much as you abandon to God, so much He will become
to you;
No less and no more will He help you out of trouble.)

The concept of "abandonment" appears to be one of complete passivity. If an individual resigns himself to God, God will come to meet him. Moreover, there seems to be expressed here a scale of possible approximations to the divine state, directly proportional to the profundity of one's resignation.

Masterpiece: The Cherubinic Wanderer

> *Wenn man GOtt reden hört.*
> Wenn du an GOtt gedänkst/ so hörstu Ihn in dir:
> Schweigstu/ und wärest still'/ Er redte für und für (V, 330).
> (*When One Hears God Speak.*
> When you think of God, you hear Him within yourself:
> Were you silent and still, He would speak constantly.)

Silence plays an important part in this exercise. The plea to men
to cease their worldly chatter and be quiet long enough to hear the
"still, small voice" which speaks from within is common to much
highly refined religion. Here, however, the silence is set up in opposition not only to speaking but even to thinking. Thinking of
God enables God to speak within one, but a complete inner silence of the mind allows Him to speak without interruption. The
internalization of God, the insistence that the Kingdom of Heaven
is to be found within, is expressed repeatedly by Scheffler:

> *Gott findet man mit nicht-suchen.*
> Gott ist nicht hier noch da: wer jhn begehrt zufinden
> Der lass' jhm Händ' und Füss'/ und Leib uñ Seele Binden
> (I, 171).
> (*God Is Found with Non-Seeking.*
> God is not here or there. Whoever would him find
> Must seek bound hand and foot, bound body, soul, and
> mind.)
>
> [Trask, p. 25.]

In this verse the effective word again comes in the title.[31] Scheffler
once more brings his talent for astonishing, seemingly paradoxical
statement into play by stating that one finds God only by not actively seeking him. The inhabitant of this world is like a man in
quicksand; the more he struggles, the more his hands and feet are
bound by the element which threatens to engulf him, and it is
only by the most delicate movements that he can save himself.
Still better is it for him not to move at all, if there is one who will
come and save. For Scheffler there is such a one, and, as we will
see in the next group of verses, He will come and save because He
must.

(2) *God needs me.* We turn now to the most confidently opti-
mistic verses in the entire work: those which express man's impor-

tance for God. Very few other ideas does Scheffler work out with such joy. The train of thought in this matter seems to indicate a kind of genesis and growth; and for that reason we are able, for once, to give the verses in the order in which they actually occur.

> *GOtt lebt nicht ohne mich.*
> Ich weiß daß ohne mich GOtt nicht ein Nu kan leben/
> Werd' ich nicht Er muß von Noth den Geist auffgeben (I, 8).
> (*God Lives Not Without Me.*
> I know that, without me, the life of God were lost;
> Were I destroyed, he must perforce give up the ghost.)
> [Trask, p. 13.]

The whole remarkable idea is capsulated here in one of Scheffler's most famous verses. It is not difficult to see why it has attracted so much attention. Scheffler only begins a line with a statement like "I know" when he has something he wishes to say with particular firmness. Ordinarily he is more inclined to deny the possibility of knowing anything worth knowing. God cannot live a moment without me. I am His *raison d'être*, and even the rhythm, which thunders on without a caesura, especially in the first line, seems to express pride in this magnificent position. There may be a kind of wordplay in the second line: if I were not what I am, if I did not exist, God would of necessity have to give up the ghost—the Holy Ghost, that is, the part of His being whose task it is to bring salvation to men. Again and again Scheffler elaborates on this theme, beginning with the very next couplet:

> *Ich habe von Gott/ und Gott von mir.*
> Daß GOtt so seelig ist und Leben ohn Verlangen/
> Hat Er so wol von mir/ als ich von Ihm empfangen (I, 9).
> (*I Receive from God, and God from Me.*
> That God so blissful is and lives without desire,
> No less did he from me than I from him acquire.)
> [Trask, p. 14.]

The word *seelig* ("blessed") is not normally applied to God; it is rather a state of man before God. By applying it to God, the poet makes the God-I relationship reciprocal even in the blessings bestowed and indeed, as appears in the second half-line, in the very

essence of God. Thus the distance between God and man is star-
tlingly foreshortened.

> *Der Mensch ists höchste Ding.*
> Nichts dünkt mich hoch zu seyn: Ich bin daß höchste Ding/
> Weil auch GOtt ohne mich Ihm selber ist gering (I, 204).
> *(Man Is the Highest Thing.*
> I count naught high; I am the highest thing of all.
> Why? Because, without me, even God himself is small.)
> [Trask, p. 29.]

Here a view of man is preached which is in startling contrast to
the demand for self-abnegation found elsewhere.[32] The importance
of man in creation here comes as close as the mystical tradition
will allow to the unique centrality of man in the account given in
Genesis; but only in general terms, for lying behind this whole
series of epigrams is the assumption of ultimate, or at any rate,
ideal, unity of God and man. Nevertheless, the existence of man in
his created form seems to shed a meaning on the existence of God.

In the following verse Scheffler finds another effective expression to press the matter of union with God:

> *GOttes ander-Er.*
> Ich bin Gotts ander-Er/ in mir findt Er allein
> Was Ihm in Ewigkeit wird gleich und ähnlich seyn (I, 278).
> *(God's Other Self.*
> I am God's other self; He findeth but in me
> His equal and His like for all eternity.)
> [Trask, p. 37.]

Here the idea of man made in God's image is taken quite seriously. The individual in his highest mystical state becomes an
alter ego of God. It seems as though the gap between man and
God were progressively closing and the otherness of man shrink-
ing in its dimensions.

Scheffler's imaginative use of traditional symbols and ideas can
be impressive when he has his heart in an issue:

> *Der eingemenschte GOtt.*
> GOtt trinkt der Menschheit Milch/ läst seiner GOttheit
> Wein:

Wie solt' er dañ numehr nicht gar durchMenschet seyn?
(III, 11).
(*The Humanized God.*
God drinketh mankind's milk, refusing Godhood's wine;
Why should he then not be a humanized Divine?)
[Bilger, p. 85.]

The couplet is a difficult one, and the translation of the first line is not entirely certain. In the mystical tradition, the idea of the *vermenschter Gott* ("God become man")[33] is expanded from the symbol of God incarnate in Christ to a wider meaning which applies to the individual. The "humanized" God is seen here drinking the milk of mankind, having apparently left behind, for the time being, the nobler wine of His higher existence (the symbol of the wine is of course borrowed from the Eucharist). At the same time Scheffler makes effective use of the possibilities of word formation which lie within the German language: he stretches usage with the word *eingemenscht* ("turned into man") and *durchMenschet* ("permeated with man") to give us the reverse of man becoming part of God, for here God fills Himself with the substance of man. Furthermore, although it is difficult in older poetry to argue from orthography, since the printer is often responsible for it, the latter form calls attention to an important feature of Scheffler's language: his compounds often do not become organic new words but remain, as it were, broken-backed, so that the process of formation and thus the continuing tension with language remains prominently on display.[34]

The very existence of man seems to place limitations on God's will:

GOtt kan nicht alls Allein.
GOtt der die Welt gemacht und wider kan zunichten:
Kan nicht ohn meinen willn die Neugeburth auß richten (III, 80).
(*God Must Have Help.*
God, who made all the world and may destroy it too,
Cannot without my will make my rebirth come true.)
[Bilger, p. 87.]

Again the idea of the individual's indispensability as the object of God's will is stressed. It will be noted that the kind of logical paradox which appears to delimit the omipotence of God does not disturb Scheffler. Whatever needs to be said to stress the point at issue and put it in an unaccustomed light will be said regardless of wider implications.

> GOtt wird ich/ weil ich vor Er war.
> GOtt wird was ich itz bin/ nimt meine Menschheit an:
> Weil ich vor Er gewest/ drumb hat er es gethan (V, 259).
> (*God Becometh I Because I Aforetime Was He.*
> God doth become what now I am, assumes my manhood; what He is,
> The same aforetime I have been: therefore it is He doeth this.)
> > [Flitch, p. 132.]

Scheffler's last expression of this kind, with its peculiar grammar (*vor* + nominative), is in a way the most startling of all. His ability to ignore time, bend it and turn it back upon itself enables him to state that he existed before God. The only possible logical defense of the statement requires that we make once again the distinction between God and Godhead. The essence of man was already in Godhead before God undertook the creation. This distinction must be kept in mind as we view the next series.

(3) *Becoming and surpassing God.* It is partly because of the fact that man is so vital to God's existence that Scheffler envisions God as making a supreme effort to draw him to Him:

> GOTT-Mensch.
> Ja denkt doch Gott wird ich/ und kombt ins Elend her/
> Auf daß ich komm ins Reich/ und möge werden Er! (III, 20).
> (*God-Man.*
> But think that God becomes I, and comes here to misery,
> That I may come into the Kingdom, and become He!)

The background for such an epigram is naturally the figure of Christ, who descended into *Elend* ("misery") in order that I might be saved. The word *Elend* etymologically means "out of the land," "exile," and it is used here in juxtaposition with *Reich*, "Kingdom," as though God exiles Himself to bring man out of exile into the Kingdom. But the single event of God becoming man is generalized. In the title a kind of God-man equation is expressed, although the capitalization of *GOTT* (which may, for all we know, be the work of the printer), does not suggest equality. But the structure of the couplet itself is balanced and chiastic. In the first line God becomes I and lowers Himself to do it; in the second I comes upward into the Kingdom of Heaven and becomes He. A completely reciprocal relationship is expressed.

In speaking of the "man become God," Scheffler expands on Christian tradition:

> *Man ißt und Trinket GOtt.*
> Wenn du Vergöttet bist/ so ißt- und trinkst- du GOtt/
> (Und diß ist ewig wahr) in jedem bissen Brodt (II, 120).
> *(One Eats and Drinks God.*
> If thou art God-imbued, thou eat'st and drinkest God;
> And this is always true, in every bite of bread.)
> [Trask, p. 44.]

The idea here is simple and rather charming in its neatness. For the man in the state of *Vergöttung* every meal is a Eucharist. He is fully in contact with the universal presence of God. But the state of *Vergöttung* is not by a long way the end of the road. In a group of longer verses at the beginning of the *Cherubinic Wanderer* Scheffler carries the process further:

> *Du must was GOtt ist seyn.*
> Sol ich mein leztes End/ und ersten Anfang finden/
> So muß ich mich in GOtt/ uñ GOtt in mir ergründen.
> Und werden das was Er: Ich muß ein Schein in Schein:
> Ich muß ein Wort im Wort/ ein GOtt im GOtte seyn (I, 6).
> *(You Must Be what God Is.*
> If I am to find my final end and first beginning,
> Then I must ground myself in God, and God in me
> And become what He is: I must be a light in the light,
> I must be a word in the Word, a God in God.)

Scheffler is still speaking in terms of the reciprocal relationship, but it is now much more on a basis of equality. Here the purely mystical idea of actually becoming God, which may seem impious to the uninitiated, is expressed in a form that moves toward it by stages. But for the pious there is a more serious shock in this group:

> *Mann muß gantz Göttlich seyn.*
> HErr es genügt mir nicht/ daß ich dir Englisch diene/
> Und in Vollkommenheit der Götter für dir Grüne:
> Es ist mir vil zuschlecht/ und meinem Geist zu klein:
> Wer Dir recht dienen wil muß mehr als Göttlich seyn (I, 4).
> (*One Must Be Completely Divine.*
> Lord for me 'tis not enough that I serve You angelically
> And flourish before You in the perfection of the gods.
> For me it is much too plain, and too small for my spirit;
> He who will serve You properly must be more than divine.)

The title contains the idea expressed in I, 6, but the content of the verse goes beyond it. I am no longer a little lower than the angels. The angels are left behind as I become more than godly. This is a striking statement; will he dare to say that I must become more than God? He certainly will:

> *Man muß noch über Gott.*
> Wo ist mein Auffenthalt? Wo ich und du nicht stehen:
> Wo ist mein letztes End in welches ich sol gehen?
> Da wo man keines findt. Wo sol ich dann nun hin?
> Ich muß noch über GOtt in eine wüste ziehn (I, 7).
> (*Rise above God.*
> "Where is my residence?" Where I nor you can stand.
> "Where is the final end where I at last shall land?"
> 'Tis where no end is found: "And whither must I press?"
> Above God I must pass, into the wilderness.)
>   [Carus, p. 40.]

There is something about this sort of verse that appears almost as impudence. Scheffler was certainly aware of the danger of misunderstanding, for he added a note in explanation: "i.e., above everything which one can know of God or think about him, according to the negative view, concerning which look among the mystics." [35] As is usually the case with Scheffler's notes, this has an effect similar to that of a joke that has been explained. The exegesis he gives is indeed congruent with the view of the mystical tradition, but one gets the impression that in more sober moments Scheffler himself occasionally became frightened over what he had written in his creative fervor and felt constrained to restore orthodoxy by adding a gloss. As a matter of fact, the justification for the verse depends at least in part upon the differentiation between God and Godhead we have mentioned several times. He regards this Godhead as a "wilderness," a place empty of qualities, into which he will retire as a hermit. But the direct dramatic effect of the statement requires no justification. It is perfectly consistent with the shock tactics which characterize his best couplets. Moreover, Scheffler's courage is not yet exhausted:

> *Die Liebe zwinget GOtt.*
> Wo GOtt mich über GOtt nicht solte wollen bringen/
> So will ich Ihn dazu mit blosser Liebe zwingen (I, 16).
> *(Love Forces God.*
> If God should not want to bring me beyond God,
> Then I will force Him to it with mere love.)

Here love itself becomes a weapon with which he forces God to carry him beyond God. It is a remarkable testimony to the poet's rich imagination and highly flexible intellect. This high-hearted confidence in the relationship with God, which Scheffler himself was apparently unable to maintain for long, reflects Eckhart's contribution to the tradition and contrasts notably with the general gloominess of the intellectual atmosphere in the seventeenth century.

(4) *The nature of the mystical union.* The final stage of the mystical process, at least in so far as it can be envisioned here below, must of course also be an object of Scheffler's concern. Here, however, we are struck with a remarkable and significant phenomenon. One would expect the mystical poet to outdo himself and burst into brilliant description of this final state, which is the goal of the entire process. But now that we are actually within range of the *unio mystica,* we find that the number of verses which deal effectively with that state is quite small. In view of all we have said before of the ineffability of the true mystical state, this fact is quite consistent with the rest of the work, but one wonders also whether Scheffler himself had achieved the ultimate

mystical experience, or whether what he has to say about it is not derived from the written tradition.

Still, he does attempt to deal with it. He does not approach it primarily in a descriptive manner, nor does he permit himself to become involved in metaphysics. Neither approach would lead him to his goal, which is to arouse in his reader an appreciation of this most desirable of human possibilities. He prefers, rather, to make unusual and startling observations, which, if we may apply the language of logic to a transcendental situation, are conclusions drawn from his understanding of the mystical union toward which the whole work urges.

One of the most attractive aspects of the state of union for Scheffler is that it offers the epitome of security, which the poet, given the uncertainties of his own character, must have felt to be a strong argument in a chaotic age in which the structure of the profane world must have seemed downright absurd.

> *Der Teuffel sicht kein Licht.*
> Mensch wikle dich in GOtt/ verbirg dich in sein Liecht:
> Ich schwehre dir beym Jah/ der Teufel sicht dich nicht (II, 249).
> *(The Devil Sees No Light.*
> Man, wrap yourself in God, hide yourself in his light:
> I swear to you by Yah, the Devil will not see you.)

The contrast of light and darkness is an element deeply rooted in the ancient tradition of Christian dualism. God the Son is the "light of the world" (John 8:12); God the Father becomes the sun in Christian iconography; and God the Holy Ghost illuminates the darkness of the soul. But the regions of damnation contain "No light, but rather darkness visible." [36] Satan himself is the Prince of darkness. To achieve unity with God, then, is to flee into the light, where the powers of darkness cannot penetrate. In a wordplay effective only in German, Scheffler swears by *Jah,* the affirming principle, which is at the same time the first syllable of the Holy Name in Hebrew. [37] The security afforded by the *unio mystica* can be expressed even more forcefully:

> *Mit GOtt vereinigt seyn/ ist gut für Ewge Pein.*
> Wer GOtt vereinigt ist/ den kan Er nicht verdammen:

Er stürtze sich dann selbst mit jhm in Tod und Flam̃en (I, 97).
(To Be United with God Is Good for Eternal Pain.
Whoever is united with God He cannot damn,
Unless He plunges Himself with him into death and flames.)

The doggerel of the title, which seems to offer a panacea for the
ailing soul, is embarrassing, to be sure. But the content of the
epigram expresses a motif which occurs repeatedly in Scheffler's
verses about the relationship between God and man. When I
achieve unity with God, in effect I bind my destiny to His; for I
am a part of Him, and whatever He does for me or to me, He does
in equal measure for and to Himself. The "man become God" is
safe from damnation, for God could not condemn him without
bringing the same judgment upon Himself. This process of becoming God, of becoming *essentially* a part of the highest essence
of the universe, is central to the mystical message; and Scheffler
strives to present it not only as a commandment to obedience
through which a man is to come into harmony with the order of
things, but also as a positive, desirable good; indeed, the highest
good.

Scheffler calls into his service a charming image to illustrate the
unified state:

> *GOtt ist in und umb mich.*
> Ich bin der Gottheit Faß in welchs sie sich ergeust/
> Sie ist mein tieffes Meer das mich in sich beschleust (IV, 157).
> *(God Is in and Around Me.*
> I am the cask of the Godhead into which it pours;
> It is my deep sea which encloses me in itself.)

The image here is similar to that which illustrates God as being at
once the point that resides in one and the circle that encloses all.
Here the whole structure is fluid rather than geometric. Godhead
flows into me as though I were a cask built to contain it. At the
same time it is an ocean, and I am as a drop of water which flows
into it and becomes immediately indistinguishable as an individual drop. The image of the drop and the sea occurs several times
in the *Cherubinic Wanderer* (I, 3; III, 168; IV, 139; VI, 171–74);
and it is one of the traditional and most expressive tropes in mystical writing.[39]

[78]

At the end of the last section we spoke of the peculiar manner in which God is seen to love only himself and implied that this kind of statement looked ahead to what is perhaps the most highly refined link in this mystical chain of being. In that verse from Book V, Scheffler gives only a hint of the situation. Here he tries to spell out clearly the promise that lies at the end of the mystical road.

> *GOtt liebet sich allein.*
> Es ist gewißlich wahr/ GOtt liebet sich allein/
> Und wer sein ander-Er in seinem Sohn kan seyn (II, 45).
> (*God Loves Himself Alone.*
> It is certainly true, God loves himself alone,
> And him who can be His other self in His son.)

God's love is reserved only for those who have managed to become a part of Him, to become his "other self," but those who reside in Him in a state of union are gloriously bathed in that radiant love. To participate in God's love thus becomes the purpose of the mystic, the highest form of blessedness to which he confidently climbs; and the promise of that participation becomes the most powerful and effective element in the message of the *Cherubinic Wanderer.*

VI *Eternity*

One of the most fascinating and at the same time recalcitrant problems with which human thought has dealt is that of the infinite. The difficulty is, of course, that the infinite marks a boundary of human reason; and the history of thought is rich in attempts to grasp a concept which it cannot transcend and, as it were, observe from the other side. The infinite is an issue in religion, esthetics, mathematics, physics, and metaphysics. Expressions of infinity, the ultimate hyperbole, are used in an attempt to express the inexpressible, desperation terms which stand in place of that which is not comprehensible. Even some mathematicians have felt that the concept does violence to the purity of their discipline; and there has been much debate over the meaning of the mathematical infinite.

Infinite time is eternity, and it presents the same problems, the same resistance to comprehension, the same refusal to be placed easily into a logical context or to become purged of its paradoxes. The mystic is thus particularly interested in the concept of eternity. By and large in the tradition, however, eternity is not understood as time stretched out to an infinite length, but rather as the absence of time, of total existential stasis in which all things exist and happen at once. This concept is bound up with the mystic's concern for unity. For him plurality is an indication of incompleteness or illusion. Only in unity can perfection be found; and perfection is a quality of that which is one. Therefore if time is understood as a succession of distinct moments, it must either be imperfect or unreal, or both; and if God is perfect, then time can not be a part of the Godhead. God may exist only in eternity, which is one single all-encompassing moment.

If Johann Scheffler is consistent with regard to any one point, it is this one. Although many of his statements on the subject are meant to be surprising and unconventional, there is no deviation from the underlying point. Time and place are unreal things of this world which obscure the true nature of God and Godhead; and a recognition of this is indispensable for the achievement of unity with God.

If we turn to the verses of the *Cherubinic Wanderer* themselves, we find once more that their order and arrangement do not help us very much. Verses on the subject are scattered more or less at random throughout the work, except in Book III; and we must move freely from book to book if we are to put Scheffler's expressions on the subject into any kind of order. The first one we shall consider, however, comes from Book I:

> *Im Grund ist alles eins.*
> Man redt von Zeit und Ort/ von Nun und Ewigkeit:
> Was ist dann Zeit und Ort/ und Nun und Ewigkeit? (I, 177).
> (*Basically All Is One.*
> Men talk of time and place, of now and eternity:
> But what are time and place and now and eternity?)
> [Trask, p. 25.]

We are perhaps inclined to be unimpressed by verse of this kind. The similarity of the two lines would seem to show a paucity of imagination, and yet there is a cleverness about them. What sounds like stupid repetition serves to hammer home the understanding that these things—time, place, now, and eternity—are in themselves stupid and meaningless. Words become hollow when they are allowed to jangle in this manner. Because of the title, we are obliged to regard the verse as a rhetorical question. The answer is: Illusion, because time and place, now and eternity appear as separate and separating qualities, whereas in reality everything is basically one. This verse is a key to the series of ideas; and all the others will expand upon it, as does the next one:

> *Die Gleichheit.*
> Ich weiß nicht was ich sol! Es ist mir alles Ein/
> Orth/ Unorth/ Ewigkeit/ Zeit/ Nacht/ Tag/ Freud/ und Pein
> (I, 190).
> (*Sameness.*
> I know not what to do! All things are one to me:
> Place, Unplace, Day, Night, Joy, Pain, Time, Eternity.)
> [Flitch, p. 164.]

The agreement between the Baroque form and the content of the couplet is happily achieved here. The first half-line reads almost as a cry of helplessness. It may not make sense to me, but I am obliged to regard these things, these opposites as one thing; and the following list of nouns, piled up in a heap of pairs in a characteristic Baroque line, is expressive of the splintering effect these false concepts have in contrast to the unity of the one.

In Book II we find another verse that expresses a lack of Scheffler's normal assuredness:

> *Die Ewigkeit.*
> Was ist die Ewigkeit? Sie ist nich diß/ nicht das/
> Nicht Nun/ nicht Ichts/ nicht Nichts/ sie ist/ ich weiß nicht was
> (II, 153).
> (*Eternity.*
> What is Eternity? It is not That, not This,
> Not Now, not Aught, not Naught—I know not what it is.)
> [Flitch, p. 158.]

This is an expression of the first emotion felt by the thinker, especially the mystic thinker, when faced with the infinite: that it is inexpressible and incomprehensible, that the nearest one can come is to find refuge in negative terms, to put it in the realm of the excluded middle by saying "not aught, not naught." And yet the resignation of the final half-line suggests an awareness that this is an unsatisfactory way of approaching something which is a keystone of existence. But Scheffler is not always overcome by this feeling of insuperable ignorance expressed in "I know not what it is."

> *Die Zeit ist Ewigkeit.*
> Zeit ist wie Ewigkeit/ und Ewigkeit wie Zeit/
> So du nur selber nicht machst einen unterscheid (I, 47).
> (*Time Is Eternity.*
> Eternity is time and time eternity.
> Except when we ourselves would make them different be.)
> [Carus, p. 39.]
> *Die Zeit und Ewigkeit.*
> Du sprichst: Versetze dich auß Zeit in Ewigkeit.
> Ist dann an Ewigkeit und Zeit ein unterscheid? (I, 188).
> (*Time and Eternity.*
> From Time into Eternity thou tellest me to get me hence!
> Between Eternity and Time is there then any difference?)
> [Flitch, p. 162.]

These verses are very similar and must be regarded together. Time and eternity are the same; only I, as a man bound to earthly things, make a difference between them. The second is a little more startling, since even part of the traditional mystical message —betake yourself from time into eternity—is described here as meaningless. But this does not mean that we may use the words interchangeably and speak of time when we should be speaking of eternity. Where there is confusion, it is caused by man himself, as we see in the couplet following directly upon the last one:

> *Der Mensch der macht die Zeit.*
> Du selber machst die Zeit: daß Uhrwerk sind die sinnen:
> Hemstu die Unruh nur/ so ist die Zeit von hinnen (I, 189).
> (*Man Makes Time.*
> Yourself you make the time, your senses are the clock.
> You stop the balance wheel, and time at once you block.
> [Carus, p. 34.]

This couplet contains the most brilliant pun in Scheffler's writings. The word *Unruh* means, normally, "unrest." It is the condition of the human being attached to nonessentials, to the constantly unstable realm of separate qualities. It is this unrest in men which Eckhart's stunning sermons tried to meet; and in the mystical tradition it has always been the characteristic of the man outside his place in God. But *Unruh* is also the technical term for the balance wheel of a clock and is used in this couplet with perfect pertinence. Unrest and the sense of time are bound together. If one puts a brake on the balance wheel of one's inner clock, stopping the sense of time, the unrest caused by the senses will cease also.

Before going on we may pause for a moment on the less tenuous and somewhat more superficial ground of Book VI, where the idea of eternity developed so far is translated into more easily recognizable homiletic form.

> *Die Ewigkeit wird für nichts geschätzt.*
> O Thorheit/ umb die zeit wagt man sich biß inn Tod!
> Und auf die Ewigkeit setzt man nur einen Spott! (VI, 18).
> (*Eternity Is Considered Nothing.*
> Oh folly! Man will strive for time unto his death
> Yet for eternity will never waste a breath!)
> > [Bilger, p. 123.]
>
> *Der gröste Narr.*
> Du schlägst umbs Zeitliche das Ewig' in den wind:
> Richt'/ ob die Welt auch wol einn größeren Narren findt?
> (VI, 19).
> (*The Greatest Fool.*
> For temporal things you throw the eternal to the winds;
> Judge whether the world can find a greater fool?)

These verses do not measure up to the preceding ones in depth of poetic power. The point expressed here, however, is enlightening. Time and eternity are not in fact the same thing in all respects. Time is evidently a distorted concept, which is carved out of the oneness of eternity; and one throws eternity to the winds if one loses oneself too much in the illusions of time.

It cannot be emphasized too often that the purpose of the Cherubinic Wanderer is to lead us upward to God, and so, having been introduced by him to the problem of eternity, we can follow our guide as the relevance of this idea to the issue of unity with God becomes more apparent:

> *Die Ewigkeit.*
> Im Fall dich länger dünkt die Ewigkeit als Zeit:
> So redestu von Peyn und nicht von Seeligkeit (II, 258).
> (*Eternity.*
> In case you think eternity is longer than time,
> Then you are speaking of torment and not of blessedness.)

To speak of a sense of humor in Scheffler's writing would be difficult; but there is occasionally a faint ironic touch in his terse tone, of which the above is an example. The matter is, however, serious. Eternity is long only for the damned. Another variation appears in Book V:

> *In der Höll ist keine Ewigekeit.*
> Betracht' es eigentlich: bey Gott ist Ewigkeit/
> Beym Teuffel in der Höll da ist ein' ewge Zeit (V, 74).[39]
> (*There Is No Eternity in Hell.*
> Consider it actually: with God there is eternity,
> With the Devil in Hell there is an eternal time.)

The distinction between eternity and eternal time is made explicit here. The damned are forbidden the perfection which is in unity. Their lot is the sufferings of time rather than the blessedness of eternity.

Before we accustom ourselves too comfortably to this complex of ideas, however, we note that Scheffler turns it around in a characteristic manner:

> *Zeit ist edler alß Ewigkeit.*
> Die Zeit ist edeler alß tausend Ewigkeiten:
> Ich kan mich hier dem Herrn/ dort aber nicht bereiten (V, 125).
> (*Time Nobler Than Eternity.*
> Time's of more use to me than great eternities;
> Here and not there prepare I God to please.
> [Bilger, p. 135.]

Although the title of this epigram may surprise us, there is something pleasing about the affirmation of life it expresses (the translation, by the way, weakens the hyperbole of the original, especially in the first line). The mystical tradition is by no means restricted, or even primarily inclined, to sour denial of the world. William James, in a lecture on mysticism, speaks of a "denial based on a deeper yes." [40] Nor is the particular view with regard to the value of life in this world original with Scheffler. In the *Theologia Deutsch* we read: "Thus is everything that exists indeed the outskirts of the eternal and of eternity, and especially that which one can know and perceive in the temporal sphere and temporal things and the creatures about God and eternity. For the creatures are an indication and a way to God and to eternity. Thus then all this is an outwork and suburb of eternity; and therefore it may well be called a paradise and be so as well." [41] Life in this world is certainly subordinate to life in God; but on the other hand it is in fact a creation of God and deserves respect as such.

To come to God Himself and His relation to eternity, we turn back to Book I:

> *GOtt ist ein Ewges Nun.*
> Ist GOtt ein Ew'ges Nun/ was fället dann darein/
> Daß Er nicht schon in mir kan alls in allem seyn? (I, 133).
> (*God Is an Eternal Now.*
> If God is an eternal now, what should interfere
> That He even in me could be all in all?)

This is one of the most striking of Scheffler's epigrams, partly because of the significance of the title phrase. Now God is identified with eternity, which is an eternal moment, an eternal now, without before and after; and because of this unity, which is one of God's defining characteristics, He can be everything in everything even when He resides within me.

> *GOtt redt am wenigsten.*
> Niemand redt weniger als GOtt ohn Zeit und ort;
> Er spricht von Ewigkeit nur bloß Ein Eintzigs Wort (IV, 129).
> (*God Speaks the Least.*
> No one speaks less than God without time and place;
> He speaks from all eternity merely a single word.)

Scheffler's knowledge of the Bible is, of course, intimate, and this is an example of it. From the moment when the command of God countermands Nathan's approval of David's desire to build a house for the Lord (II Sam. 7), the Word of God becomes more and more an operating entity in its own right, this tradition carries into New Testament times (John 1:1), where John's *logos* appears again in the full force of its meaning and mystery. Eternity is but one moment, and God utters but one sound, one word, to express His existence in it.

> *GOtt siht nichts zuvor.*
> Gott sihet nichts zuvor: Drumb leugstu wenn du ihn
> Mit der Vorsehung mißt nach deinem blöden Sinn (V, 92).
> (*God Foreseeth Nothing.*
> God forsees nothing—'tis thy dull and blundering sense
> Doth clothe Him with the attribute of Providence.)
> [Flitch, p. 104.]

The surprise quality of this verse lies in its denial of a commonly accepted premise; that God is omniscient and therefore knows the future. But the concept of "future" makes no sense in the context we have been discussing; and Scheffler makes this clear in an appended note: "In God there is no looking ahead or back, but rather He sees from all eternity everything present before Him, as it happens, not as it will happen or has happened." [42] This note makes the matter unambiguously clear: eternity is one moment. For God everything happens at once, and He knows everything at once. Those who think of Him in terms of prescience are therefore detracting from the majesty of the unity which He is and in which He participates. The language of the second line supports this; Scheffler uses the verb *messen*, "to measure"; and even the application of such an attribute as prescience to God is to measure and thus delimit Him in an inadmissible way.

The following verse unifies a number of the concepts Scheffler is trying to bring to our attention:

> *Wo die Zeit am längsten.*
> Je weiter man von GOtt/ je tieffer in der Zeit:
> Drumb ist den Höllischen ein Tag ein' Ewigkeit (V, 341).
> (*Where Time Is Longest.*
> The farther one is from God, the deeper he is in time;
> Therefore for those in Hell a day is an eternity.)

Masterpiece: The Cherubinic Wanderer

The more one buries oneself in the time of this world and its illusions, the farther one moves from God. But turning one's face
away from God is sin, and the complete absence of God is Hell.
So it comes that in the state of Hell eternity disappears altogether
and each day becomes an eternity. This contrasts nicely with V,
74, quoted above. That verse expresses what is essentially the
same idea but in different terms. There is no eternity in Hell, only
eternal time. This cross-play of different words and phrases tend-
ing to the same point or, indeed, of the same word having here
the normal meaning, there a transcendental one, is typical of
Scheffler as one of the methods by which he calls our attention to
the words we use and at the same time tries to break down the
barriers they erect.

In concluding this section, we turn to one of the most difficult of
Scheffler's verses in this work:

> *Wer älter ist als GOtt.*
> Wer in der Ewigkeit mehr lebt als einen Tag/
> Derselbe wird so Alt/ als GOtt nicht werden mag (II, 33).
> *(He Who Is Older than God.*
> Whoever lives in eternity more than one day,
> He becomes older than God may become.)

The title, as is often the case, presents a startling statement, which
one expects the verse to clarify; but the meaning of the verse is
not immediately apparent. One may say, first of all, that again the
primary intention of the verse is to shock the reader into a contemplation of the problem. Sober consideration comes later; and
by that time the verse has done its work. There is a sense to the
epigram, too, however. To demand from eternity more than one
day—Scheffler might as well have said one moment (one fears the
"day" is there for the sake of the rhyme)—is to demand more than
God himself may have. It is a way of saying that he who tries to
make eternity into days following days destroys the unified Godhead which eternity reflects. In any case the expression is sophisticated and one of the Scheffler's most penetrating epigrams.

We have followed, not what we reconstruct to be necessarily
Scheffler's train of thought, but a possible order of the verses,
which takes us from an opening question regarding the nature of
eternity to the fullest expression of its meaning with regard to the

union with God. We have seen how the poet sets infinite time against worldly time, so that this polarity itself becomes a symbol of the distinction between the imperfect character of this world and the all-encompassing oneness of the divinity which is superior to it. We have seen, too, a little of the method by which Scheffler's art attempts to make these matters accessible to the limited perception of man. We shall now turn to one more vital problem in the religious complex and see how Scheffler draws from his tradition to cope with it.

VII *Death*

Few human concerns are as universal as death. Its very inevitability fastens upon the imagination. It stands as a fearful threat of meaninglessness in the face of all human hope and striving. It is, therefore, obvious that it is an important object of concern for two of man's most profound spiritual activities: religion and poetry. Religion is obliged to deal with death in some fashion or other. It can accept death, embrace it, deny it, explain it away, but it cannot ignore it. Tough-minded moderns have bitterly criticized religion, or at least the Christian tradition, for circumventing the grim reality of death as a sop to men who cannot bear the thought that their priceless individual existence will one day be snuffed out forever.

Be that as it may, it is certainly true that the mystic does not regard death as the modern rationalist would have him do; and whereas the mystic's acceptance of death has a positive element not unlike that urged by Schopenhauer and Nietzsche, it is based upon a preliminary denial. For the mystic, death, as it is commonly understood, is not a reality. More than having conquered the fear of death, he stands in astonishment before men who can have such a fear. He faces death, reaches out toward it, and joyfully embraces it, for it is his gateway to the dearly desired goal. When he tries to talk to the world about it, he is placed in a difficult position; it is not easy for him to empathize with others, but if he is a mystic writer, he may try to annihilate the specter of death in the imagination of his fellow men by a bombardment of words.

For the poet, the universality of the concept of death is reflected in the various possibilities of dealing with it. Death can, for example, stand on either side of a symbolic or metaphorical equation. Death symbols are well-known and reach far back into the history of literature. On the other hand, death as a symbol for something else, for rebirth, for the continuity of creation, is a familiar poetic image.[43] Scheffler is not precisely in the latter position, but for him also the concept of death has two facets; and it is important to distinguish just which he means when he speaks of it. The most immediate meaning is the ordinary one: common, everyday death, the refusal of the flesh to function any longer. That Scheffler discusses death in this way may be evidence that he is not so thoroughly absorbed in mystical ideas as to have lost contact with the basic attitudes of men. But in his finest and most mystical verses, death signifies something quite different. It is a spiritual death, a dying away from the world and the flesh with all its vanities, a death of I-ness, of the ego, even of the individual soul, which is carried up into the higher universal life of union with God.

Having said this, we may now proceed to organize some of Scheffler's verses which deal with death into a scheme which attempts to separate these ideas. It is important to note, as in the preceding section, that we are not pretending to follow Scheffler's own spiritual development on the subject, about which we know nothing. We shall be placing the verses in an order of development which is by no means chronological. We shall begin, therefore, with the verses in which it appears that Scheffler deals with death in the ordinary sense, then discuss a transitional group, and finally discuss those in which the problem of spiritual death is the subject.

(1) *Death as the ordinary concept.* If the view that, in the later books of the *Cherubinic Wanderer* Scheffler becomes less of a mystic and more of a Catholic theologian, were strictly true, we should expect to find the majority of these verses toward the end of the collection. That they are not remarkable by any such tendency shows that this view is not always helpful when we seek to organize the work into approachable units. However, for the first, and least impressive, of these verses, we shall reach into Book IV, written, according to Ellinger,[44] during Scheffler's period of indecision between Protestantism and Catholicism.

Der Tod ist gut und böse.
So gut der Tod auch ist dem der im HErren stirbt/
So ungut ist er dem/ der ausser jhm verdirbt (IV, 105).
    (Death Is Good and Bad.
As good as death is for him who dies in the Lord,
So bad it is for him who perishes outside of Him.)

This verse, which appears in a series of epigrams on the subject of
death (IV, 101–6), captures our attention because of its very
commonplace character. Death is good for the faithful; it is bad
for the wicked. As a Christian thought it is quite in order; as a
mystical spur for the purpose of exciting us to an unbelief in, or
desire for, death, it is ineffective. Moving back into Book II, we
find the following epigram:

Todt und GOtt.
Tod ist der Sünden Sold; Gott ist der Tugend Lohn:
Erwürbstu diesen nicht/ so trägstu den darvon (II, 29).
    (Death and God.
Death is the wages of sin, God is the reward of virtue;
If you do not achieve the latter, you will bear the former away.)

The couplet was obviously inspired by a familiar line from the
Bible (Rom. 6:23). It is but a statement of the doctrine of reward
and punishment. But poetically it is a little more interesting than
IV, 105. The Biblical line is balanced by a second half-line in
which is stated, not that salvation is the reward of virtue, but
that it lies in possessing God Himself. There are two sets of antithetical statements, rather than one as in IV, 105. We have something which is more intense, if not more profound.

In our third example we will take a small leap to a faint indication of what the mystic wants to say:

Der Tod vergöttet dich.
Wenn du gestorben bist/ und GOtt dein Leben worden/
So trittstu erst recht ein der Hoben Götter Orden (I, 34).
    (Death Turns You into God.
When you are dead, and God has become your life,
Then you will really enter into the order of the high gods.)

[90]

Here we are not reaching quite to God; but we are promised admission to the "order of the high gods." Whatever this may mean —it is difficult to determine when Scheffler speaks of the "gods" whether it is an undigested Classical reminiscence or a special category in the mystical scheme—it has less of a strictly Christian flavor than the preceding two epigrams. The concept of *Vergöttung,* of man becoming God, appears in the title.

Returning to Book IV, we find a more excited tone:

> *Auch von jhm* [*dem Tod*].
> Man wünschet jhm den Tod/ und fliehet jhn doch auch:
> Jens ist der Ungeduld und diß der Zagheit brauch (IV, 102).
> (*Of Death*
> A mortal yearns for death yet flees it constantly;
> Yon lies impatience's way, this way timidity.
> [Bilger, p. 47.]

Now his antithesis is speaking to us in terms we readily recognize; indeed, perhaps too readily. Shall we read out of the first half-line a psychological perception; of the death-wish? The application of psychological categories to older poetry is a delicate matter. Perhaps it is an anticipatory perception; but we will do better to interpret it mainly within the context of Scheffler's argument. He is setting up a dilemma for the radically faithful Christian who combines the longing for death with the human fear of it. Both attitudes lack the resignation required of the empty, God-filled man. The first the poet ascribes to impatience, the second to cowardice. Both are wrong.

Now we are about to make another leap, this time a longer one:

> *Der Tod ists beste Ding.*
> Ich sage/ weil der Tod allein mich machet frey;
> Daß er das beste Ding auß allen Dingen sey (I, 35).
> (*Death Is the Best Thing.*
> I do declare that death, because he makes me free,
> The best thing in the world, the very best must be.)
> [Carus, p. 170.]

We are still talking about death as it is commonly understood. The verse is not even necessarily in the realm of the transcendental. But the positiveness of it is striking: "I do declare" at the beginning is a call to attention. Death is good; indeed, it is the best of all things because it frees me from this vale of tears. The meaningfulness of such a statement lies not in what it says, which is in itself hyperbolic; it lies rather in the violent contrast to its opposite, which is the belief of everyday man that death is the worst of all things. Here Scheffler displays his fundamental method as a mystical writer, a statement almost shocking with which he hopes to neutralize the contrary belief of his reader. We shall now leave this group and go on to one which seems to build a bridge between man's everyday understanding of death and the mystical treatment of it.

(2) *Transition.* In dealing with a work of this kind, it is quite difficult and perhaps perilous to attempt to draw boundaries and make distinctions. We are trying to suggest a spectrum, set off in three main groups; and although it was not too difficult to illustrate the first one, from this point on distinctions become increasingly arbitrary. At any rate, it seems that between the verses dealing with physical death and those treating spiritual death is a group which is neither one nor the other, but participates a little in both; and these we shall look at under the heading of transition. The following couplet is offered as the first in this group because of an interesting double interpretation that can be put upon it:

> *Vom Tode.*
> Der Tod ist doch noch gutt: könt' ihn ein Höllhund haben/
> Der liss' im Augenblik sich Lebendig begraben (IV, 101).
> *(On Death.*
> Death is good after all: if a hound of Hell could have it,
> In a moment he would let himself be buried alive.)

Why? Because it would free him from the torments that even he, as a servant of Hell and one hated by God, must suffer? Or because through it he might find the way to blessedness which is closed to him? It is hard to say whether Scheffler is speaking of death as a finality, or as the first step to eternal life. The verse, however, is successful in so far as it provokes such questions.

> *Kein Todt ist ohn ein Leben.*
> Ich sag es stirbet nichts: nur daß ein ander Leben/
> Auch selbst das Peinliche/ wird durch den Tod gegeben (I, 36).

Masterpiece: The Cherubinic Wanderer

> (*No Death Without a Life.*
> I say that nothing dies; rather, another life
> By dying is bestowed, though it be lived in strife.)
>   [Bilger, p. 61.]

Nothing is particularly extraordinary about this couplet; it simply
states that Heaven or Hell is another life which follows death. But
a connection between death and life is now seen. Let us see where
this will take us:

> *Der Ewige Tod.*
> Der Tod/ auß welchem nicht ein Neues Leben blühet/
> Der ists den meine Seel auß allen Töden fliehet (I, 29).
>   (*The Eternal Death.*
> The death whence no new life doth flower nor come to be,
> Of all deaths is the death from which my soul doth flee.)
>   [Trask, p. 16.]

There seem to be, according to this, several different kinds of
death, and the poet does wish to flee the one out of which no new
life grows. Whether he means to say that there is actually such a
thing as the eternal death of which the title speaks is not clear.
The thought expressed is that the idea of death as a finality is
terrible, whether there be such a thing or not, and that one ought
to embrace and welcome death precisely because it is the source
of new life. In the couplet following the one above, Scheffler becomes even less transparent:

> *Es ist kein Tod.*
> Ich glaube keinen Tod: Sterb ich gleich alle Stunden/
> So hab ich jedesmahl ein besser leben funden (I, 30).
>   (*There Is No Death.*
> I say, there is no death. If every hour I die,
> Each time a better life has come to me thereby.)
>   [Trask, p. 17.]

The title, which categorically denies the very existence of death,
captures the reader's attention. But if there is no death, there is a
dying; and dying repeatedly will produce a better life. Here the

concept of death is already beginning to reproduce by fission, as it were, and a new element appears. What dies must be the willful self, which, in its withering away, makes room for the inflow of God. The relationship of death leading to life is now clearly internalized. Scheffler can carry this relationship still further:

> *Das Leben und der Tod.*
> Kein Tod ist herrlicher als der ein Leben bringt:
> Kein Leben edler/ als das auß dem Tod entspringt (IV, 103).
> > (*Life and Death.*
> No death is more magnificent than that which brings life;
> No life nobler than that which arises from death.)

Scheffler here elaborates on the previous intimation of the different kinds of death expressed in I, 29. Death out of life, life out of death, is expressed with an unqualified positiveness. The range of nuances in the words used is becoming broader. The positive quality is even stronger in a verse in which Scheffler affirms life with a rare enthusiasm:

> *Verlust und Gewinn.*
> Der Tod ist mein Gewinn/ Verlust das lange Leben:
> Und dennoch dank ich GOtt daß er mir diß gegeben.
> Ich wachs' und nehme zu/ so lang ich hier noch bin:
> Darumb ist auch gar wol daß Leben mein Gewin (IV, 132).
> > (*Loss and Gain.*
> Death is my gain, long life is loss,
> And still I thank God that he has given me this.
> I grow and expand, as long as I am here;
> Therefore even life is indeed my gain.)

Of Scheffler's four-line verses, this is one of the best. In terms of the disdainful view of the world, which is characteristic of him and particularly noticeable in Book IV, the antithetical turn in the middle of the second line comes as a considerable surprise, and yet it makes perfectly good sense. As a terse inspirational expression, it competes with the two-line verses in a way that few of the longer ones are able to do. In addition, it is one of those verses which one can, if one is so minded, lift completely out of its particular religious context and give it a more modern relevance. It is true that to do this would be to do violence to Scheffler's intention; but this kind of multivalence is one of the qualities that keep poetry alive from age to age.

Before leaving this group, we shall look at one verse that points the way toward the third set:

> GOtt sterben und GOtt leben.
> Stirb oder leb in GOtt; du thust an beiden wol:
> Weil man GOtt sterben muß und GOtt auch leben sol (II, 58).
> (*Dying God and Living God.*
> Die or live in God: you do well with both.
> Because one must die God, and should live God as well.)

This couplet does not yield its meaning as easily as most. The phrases "die God" and "live God" violate grammatical idiom, and consequently they lie near that outer periphery of language where the mystic attempts to mediate somehow between the rational and the irrational. But the couplet is successful, and the phrase in question expresses a more profound unity than the dying and living "in God" which appears in the first line. The relationship has been tightened up. As a result the mystical undertone is more perceptible. We shall have occasion to return to this verse before long.

(3) *Spiritual death.* We have now to deal with our last grouping in what is really an extended attempt to approach what Scheffler means when he talks about death. Before saying anything about spiritual death, or about *Absterben,* the inner dying away of the self, let us look at a couplet from Book II

> *Nichts lebet ohne Sterben.*
> GOtt selber/ wenn er dir wil leben/ muß ersterben:
> Wie dänckstu ohne Tod sein Leben zuererben? (I, 33).
> (*Nothing Lives without Death.*
> God Himself, if He will live for you, must die;
> How can you inherit His life without death?)

Here we are clearly in another realm. The title still reflects that relationship between death and life of which we have spoken before. The second line appears at first sight to mean only that one must die to inherit eternal life. But looking at it more closely, one realizes the significance of "His life." We are no longer simply dying into another life in the beyond, but into *God's* life. The death of God in the first line refers, of course, to the sacrifice of Christ, but Scheffler carefully puts it into the present tense (to be sure, the past tense would have created a metrical problem, as Scheffler regularly apocopates final -*e* only before vowels), thus turning the death of God into a continual process repeated for each person and requiring reciprocally his death in order to reach Him.

Let us now go to an extreme in the matter of spiritual death, a four-line verse from Book III which shows how violent Scheffler can sometimes become.

> *Der Haß seiner selbst.*
> Ich lieb und hasse mich/ ich führe mit mir Kriege/
> Ich brauche List und Macht/ daß ich mich selbst besiege:
> Ich schlag' und tödte mich/ ich mach' es wie ich kan
> Daß ich nicht ich mehr bin: rath was ich für ein Mann? (III, 229).
> *(The Hatred of Himself.*
> I love and hate myself, I wage war with myself:
> I use cunning and strength, that I may defeat myself:
> I beat and kill myself, I do whatever I can
> That I may be no longer I: guess what sort of man I am?)

The ascetic self-destructiveness contained in these verses is not in good repute among modern men. Scheffler, both in his way of life and in many of his verses, was more inclined to it than many of his great mystical forebears. Even Suso, it will be remembered, reportedly gave up the life of self-mortification at what he understood to be a divine command. The asceticism, however, is not preached here in the physical sense; it is transferred into the realm of the spirit. In a quite effective verse, the military metaphor is consistently carried through the first three lines, and the last half-line puts a rhetorical question directly to the reader, who is obliged to measure his stature as a Christian against the intensity of the effort portrayed. The tension between love and hate for self posed in the first half-line creates a sense of the difficulty of extinguishing one's own self, which undoubtedly was part of Scheffler's own troubled experience. This type of violent expression occurs again in a late verse:

> *Man muß getödtet seyn.*
> Alls muß geschlachtet seyn. Schlachstu dich nicht für GOtt/
> So schlachtet dich zu letzt fürn Feind der ewge Tod (VI, 193).
> (*One Must be Killed.*
> Everything must be slaughtered. If you do not slaughter yourself
> for God,
> Then finally eternal death will slaughter you for Satan.)

This couplet is an example of the rhetoric of terror which is not so prominent in the earlier books of the *Cherubinic Wanderer* but which plays an important role in the later *Sensual Description of the Four Last Things* and in some of the polemic tracts. The threefold use of the word "slaughter," especially in the categorical statement in the first half-line, is calculated to arouse fear. Its use stresses emotionally the inevitability of death, over which I must get some sort of control. I must kill myself for God, kill the I-ness within me. If I do not master the forces of death and apply them to my inner self, then they will get out of hand and deliver me up to the Devil.

At this point we shall turn to something quite different:

> *Der allerseeligste Tod.*
> Kein Tod ist seeliger/ als in dem HErren sterben/
> Und umb das Ewge Gutt mit Leib und Seel verderben (I, 28).
> (*The Most Blessed Death.*
> No death is more blessed than to die in the Lord
> And perish with body and soul for the eternal possession.)

The tone here is quiet and has become more passive. Indeed, except for one thing—that the *soul* must perish, a concept which is clearly mystical—it is indistinguishable from a remark by any uninspired preacher. We shall see more of this presently, but first let us see what God's part in this process is. Among the transitional verses we noted, in II, 58, Scheffler's statement about living and dying God. Now the relationship of subject and predicate is shifted once more, so that God appears to do these things:

> *GOtt stirbt und lebt in uns.*
> Ich sterb' und leb' auch nicht: GOtt selber stirbt in mir:
> Und was ich leben sol/ lebt Er auch für und für (I, 32).
> (*God Dies and Lives in us.*

Neither do I die and live; God Himself dies in me:
And what I should live, He lives also continually)

The vision of the crucified Christ is always in the background in this sort of expression. But the standpoint is unusual. Here I no longer die and live myself; it is God functioning in me who does these things. Despite some scholastic comments added to this verse by Scheffler later, when he was more interested in logic and apologetics,[45] its power lies in its remarkably successful attempt to catch hold of the inexpressible, the unity with God. He lives and dies in me, because I have managed to kill the I which normally does these things.

We spoke in connection with I, 28, of the dying away of the soul. Here we shall see an expression of this remarkable doctrine founded on a word of Jesus:

> Der herrliche Tod.
> Christ/ der ist herrlich todt/ der allem abgestorben/
> Und jhm dadurch den Geist der armuth hat erworben (IV, 214).
> (The Magnificent Death.
> Christian, he is magnificently dead who has died away from all,
> And has thereby won himself the spirit of poverty.)

Here Scheffler, close to the Bible as always, takes hold of the first Beatitude, "Blessed are the poor in spirit" (Matt. 5:3). The expression is unmistakable: one must die away from everything, even from the individuality of the spirit and soul. Everything in me that is rooted in I-ness must die before I can reach unity with God. My soul, too, in so far as it is mine, with its own character, must die away. I must strive for the spirit of poverty, which means to be poor in spirit. This idea is summed up in a fine terse statement in Book V:

> Der Ichheit Tod/ stärckt in dir Gott.
> So viel mein Ich in mir verschmachtet und abnimbt/
> So viel deß Herren Ich darfür zu kräfften kömbt (V, 126).
> (The Death of I-Hood Strengthens God in Thee.
> The more the I in me doth fail, diminish and sink lower,
> So much the more the I of God aggrandizeth its power.)
> [Flitch, p. 134.]

The words here applied to the individual I—"languish" and "dete-riorate" are better in this context than Flitch's "diminish" and "sink lower"—finally apply the concept of a spiritual death in its most characteristic mystical sense. This radical confrontation with self-will, expressed here in its clearest form, sheds light on all the verses we have discussed in this section, even on those which appear to be conventional homilies upon death. All life, and all death, can be bathed in the mystical vision.

VIII *Conclusion*

Despite the existence of many useful studies, scholarship has not yet said the final word on the *Cherubinic Wanderer*. There is still much to be gained by the application of modern techniques of interpretation to Scheffler's verse; and there is need for more order in our understanding of the intellectual and religious land-scape over which the work ranges. It is likely, however, that even such additional study will not bring us much closer to a compre-hension of the personality hidden behind the work. It occasionally has been remarked that there is a certain incongruence in the work as a whole which is of a different kind than any real or apparent paradox in the use of language in the verses themselves. Günther Müller has claimed that the use of the strict Alexandrine form for the purpose of mystical speculation is in itself a para-dox.[46] This may be an overstatement, although in one sense it can be argued that the free flow of prose is more suitable to mysticism in so far as the sheer artifice of bound forms has an alienating effect upon the substance of the message. On the other hand, it is apparent that the irrational and transcendental qualities of poetry have a part to play in the mystical realm. Baumgardt says with justice that "we do not degrade mysticism by putting it in close proximity to poetry." [47] In the specific case of the *Cherubinic Wanderer*, however, it is the effect of the work as a whole which stands in a rather disturbing contrast to the mystical message. On the one hand, the scattershot technique of short, often startling verses, which are thrust upon the reader without any apparent order, is intended to serve the development of the metalinguistic mystical experience; on the other, this technique radiates nervous-ness and lack of inner peace and equilibrium instead of mystical abandonment, struggle instead of quietude, and, ultimately, doubt instead of certainty. This unease doubtlessly reflects a major disharmony in Scheffler's personality. Though more poet than theologian, he cared more about religion than he did about poetry.

For these reasons, and from our knowledge of Scheffler's subsequent career, the conclusion appears irresistible that Scheffler's mysticism was intellectual rather than experiential and emotional, that its ultimate source lies in the letter of the tradition instead of in the overwhelming personal experience which is the mark of the true mystic. This observation would apply as well to the less dialectical, "Seraphic" *Holy Joy of the Soul.* This can best be illustrated by a topic which is of particular interest to the modern reader. It was one of Eckhart's great achievements that he directed attention away from the frenzied insistence of the various orders and sects of his time upon the "right" way to grace and salvation and toward the inwardness of religious experience. He was willing to allow men to find God in their own way, so long as the way led to an abandonment of self-will and a recognition of the ultimate unity. This limited but real form of tolerance finds expression in a series of four couplets in the *Cherubinic Wanderer* (I, 266–69), of which the following will serve as an example:

> *Dem Spötter tauget nichts.*
> Ich weiß die Nachtigal strafft nicht des GukGuks thon:
> Du aber/ sing ich nicht wie du/ sprichst meinem Hohn (I, 266).
> (*Nothing Hath Worth for the Scorner.*
> The Nightingale mocks not the Cuckoo's note, 'tis true,
> And yet you scorn my song if I sing not as you.)
> [Flitch, p. 211.]

The couplet reads well to the modern ear; it seems to erase distinctions between one religious form and another by arguing an equality between the sounds men make in their spiritual efforts. In the next two couplets (I, 267, 268), Scheffler calls attention to the fact that harmony is a combination of different voices. God will be pleased with a chorus of various attempts at religious life and expression. Why, indeed, should Scheffler not say this, since it was the intolerance of a narrow-minded censor for a different voice which plunged him into a major crisis? Yet finally we are forced to believe that the couplet is an expression of an idea from the mystical tradition, not the reflection of an innate trait of character; for in his final stage Scheffler explicitly and violently fought the principle of tolerance in every way he could.

Whatever one's reservations in this matter, the *Cherubinic Wanderer* remains a recognized masterpiece of German literature, and it was not without its influence. Scheffler's work stands on the boundary between the medieval mystical tradition and the Pietism which was to play such an important role in eighteenth-century German culture. In 1701, the seminal Pietist theologian Gottfried Arnold (1666–1730) republished the work, along with an intelligent and appreciative introduction,[48] thus introducing it into the Protestant tradition, where it was also imitated.[49] The philosopher Leibniz, who saw in the *Cherubinic Wanderer* pantheistic elements that reminded him of Spinoza, adverted to it several times.[50] In the nineteenth century, Angelus Silesius caught the attention of a number of people,[51] including the eclectic *littérateur* Karl August Varnhagen von Ense, who published excerpts from the *Cherubinic Wanderer* in 1820 and again in 1834 with notes by his clever wife Rahel,[52] and the greatest of Romantic critics, Friedrich Schlegel, who wrote an essay on the work in 1819.[53] Among writers in Germany, the work was uncommonly fruitful; Friedrich Rückert (1788–1866) modeled some of his own verses on those of Scheffler;[54] and the Westphalian poetess Annette von Droste-Hülshoff, a tense and religious personality herself, in 1835 wrote a poem in Alexandrines using the idiom of the *Cherubinic Wanderer*.[55] Nor was the interest in Angelus Silesius confined to writers who remained within the Christian faith. Gottfried Keller (1819–90), in Book IV, Chapter 12, of *Der grüne Heinrich* (*Green Henry*, final version, 1879), skillfully wove some of Scheffler's couplets into a light conversation, where their paradoxes are seen chiefly in the light of Ludwig Feuerbach's materialism; and Thomas Mann, in *Doktor Faustus* (1947), ends a letter to the demonic composer Adrian Leverkühn from his music teacher Kretzschmar with one of Scheffler's epigrams (III, 224).[56] Finally, it is interesting that some of the verses of the Silesian son of a Polish nobleman were translated into Polish in 1836 by the greatest Romantic poet of that nation, Adam Mickiewicz (1798–1855).[57]

This record shows that the *Cherubinic Wanderer*, though it

may be derivative in its content, and somewhat lacking in profound personal experience, is nevertheless a literary achievement of the highest order, capable of winning the respect of writers of the greatest sensitivity. Indeed, of Scheffler it may be said what another great religious aphorist, Jesus ben Sirach, said of himself: "Those who understand sayings become skilled themselves, and pour forth apt proverbs" (Ecclesiasticus 18:29).

CHAPTER 3

The Bride of Jesus: Holy Joy of the Soul

I *The Tradition of Erotic Sublimation*

REGARDLESS of one's religious commitments or intellectual posture, no work of Scheffler is less accessible to the modern mind than the *Holy Joy of the Soul*. Yet it belongs to a long tradition, to what William James, in reference to St. Theresa (1515–82) called "an endless amatory flirtation . . . between the devotee and the deity." [1] In our paradoxical position as the heirs of a Christian dualism in which many of us no longer believe, we sometimes feel the religion is discredited when its mechanisms of erotic sublimation are exposed. Other ages thought differently. They were less inclined to turn their eyes away from the oppressive fact of the erotic urge than some later generations, and they tried instead to turn that urge toward higher spiritual aspirations. The Hebrew Song of Songs, a painfully beautiful poem steaming with sexual longing, found its place in the canon of three great religions because it was discovered that these passions could be harnessed to the love of God.

There is another tradition lying behind the work, one which is, characteristically enough, of medieval origin. In the late Middle Ages, the clergy attempted to counter the natural pleasure people found in singing worldly folk and love songs by altering their texts and giving them a religious direction, often turning the theme of love toward God or, quite frequently, toward the Virgin Mary. This parodistic technique, called *Kontrafaktur,* is traceable as far back as the thirteenth century and continued well into the sixteenth. Recently considerable attention has been given to the use which Bach made of this convention.[2] The method lives on today not only in the songs of the Salvation Army but also in the new meanings and references given to old songs by the civil rights movement in the United States. In the German seventeenth century, Scheffler's *Holy Joy of the Soul* is the most outstanding example of *Kontrafaktur,* although others, including the Jesuit poet Jakob Balde (1604–68), attempted it, and for the same reason, namely to turn the attention of men away from worldly things.

Because of the ephemeral nature of popular song, probably no one will ever know how much of it has gone through this transformation and found a place in Scheffler's work. Enough has been demonstrated to indicate that the amount is considerable. Ellinger has collected a number of such correspondences.[3] For example, the first verse of a seventeenth-century pastoral poem reads as follows:

> Jetztund kömpt die Zeit heran,
> Da ich werde schawn an,
> Meine schöne Schäfferin,
> Der ich gantz ergeben bin.
> (Now comes the time
> When I will be able to look upon
> My pretty shepherdess
> To whom I am completely devoted.)

This is what Scheffler makes of it:

> Ach wenn kömt die Zeit heran/
> Daß ich möge schauen an
> Meinen liebsten JEsum Christ/
> Der mein Lieb und Leben ist? (I, ii, stanza 1).[4]
> (O when will the time come
> That I may look upon
> My dearest Jesus Christ,
> Who is my love and life?)

It is characteristic of this sort of parodistic procedure that the meter, the rhyme scheme, and, to some extent, even the rhymes themselves of the original are maintained in the *Kontrafaktur.*

Not only folk songs but also contemporary poems undergo transformations in Scheffler's work. Scholars have identified transformed versions of poems by Martin Opitz, Johann Hermann Schein (1586–1630), Johann Franck (1618–77), Josua Stegmann (1588–1632), and Friedrich von Spee (1591–1635). This latter connection is of some interest. Spee was a Jesuit priest who lived a rather unusual life—among other things he wrote a brave book against witch-burning—and was one of the genuinely gifted poets of his time. His posthumous collection of poems with the attractive title *Trutznachtigall* (roughly, *In Defiance of the Nightingale,* 1649), also contained religious poems with erotic themes or echoes of popular songs. In this case, therefore, Scheffler does not transform the content but simply does variations on his predecessor. It must be remembered in reference to this and other features of Scheffler's writing that the concept of plagiarism barely existed during his times. Poetry was not romantically understood as the self-expression of an original personality but as a skill applied to a particular purpose.

In his introduction Scheffler is quite clear about the extraneous purposiveness of his work. In fact, in the terms in which we are accustomed to think about poetry today, he rather devalues his own work when he speaks of its "pleasant sound which can sweeten and sugar the bitterness of this world." [5] He goes on in even more self-effacing terms: "Although now in these songs I do not make use of high and magnificent speech or deep sayings, but practiced the love of my soul with simple words according to the character of my disposition[!], nevertheless I know that you will be well satisfied with it, since such love does not consist in any pomp of words, but in uprightness of the spirit and in a simple heart." [6] Here Scheffler seems to be making an implicit distinction from the more intellectual quality of the *Cherubinic Wanderer.* Scheffler goes on to inveigh against the seductiveness of worldly love poetry which misdirects the attention from eternal concerns. This is the closest he comes to indicating his borrowings from secular song and poetry; but in a note appended to the introduction it is remarked that the melodies, which were also printed with the poems, composed by one Georg Joseph,[7] were partly not original.[8]

The long, informative title of the work, typical of the period, begins: *Holy Joy of the Soul, Or Spiritual Shepherd-Songs of Psyche in Love with her Jesus.* The familiar image of Jesus as the shepherd of men allows the connection to the conventions of pastoral love poetry. Psyche, the soul (a conveniently feminine noun), languishes ecstatically in her love and longing for Jesus. In the first three books, the succession of poems follows the progress of the liturgical year, beginning with Advent. Thus Book I proceeds from intense longing for the Redeemer to ecstatic greeting of the newborn Child coupled in a curious way with the happiness of the Bridegroom. Book II deals largely with the Passion, and the third book treats the Resurrection and the Ascension, followed by new longing, which is resolved by unity in the Eucharist. The liturgical year thus completed, the fourth book reworks some of the motifs from the first three in a somewhat scattered fashion and adds some new figures belonging to the general theme of love for Jesus, such as Mary, John, and Mary Magdalene. In the first edition of the work the fourth book was printed separately and may actually have been composed some time after the first three.

The *Holy Joy of the Soul* is a virtuoso performance of a different kind from that of the *Cherubinic Wanderer*. In the latter work the poet rings the changes on a single metrical form, the rugged Alexandrine, with a mastery which can be matched in its consistency only by Andreas Gryphius and Friedrich von Logau. In this work, on the other hand, one is struck by the wide variety of metrical and strophic forms, demonstrating a lyrical range on Scheffler's part which one would not have suspected from the *Cherubinic Wanderer*. From simple four-line stanzas of rhymed couplets through the larger eight-line stanzas familiar from the Protestant hymn, to involved forms with internal rhymes and shifting meters, the collection is nearly an encyclopedia of the lyrical forms available to German poetry at that time.[9]

Even if one is willing to tolerate as valid the principle of religious eroticism, there is a great danger lurking in the genre. Because the erotic urge has been turned to purposes which *ipso facto* require no apology, certain restraints still operative in love poetry as such may show a tendency to dissolve. If one may say so: the irresponsibility of the position in which the poet places himself, that he is and is not writing love poems, requires considerable esthetic discipline on his part to avoid a number of quite proximate pitfalls. The erotic imagery can become overheated. Too much strain can be put on the assumption that sensual images are to be understood in a spiritual sense. There can occur a superfluity of tropic epithet. The yearning can become maudlin and the interaction of love flirtatious or prissy. Above all, the danger of a trivialization of religious experience and of Jesus himself is constantly present. All of these things happen in the *Holy Joy of the Soul*. Along with them there are some passages astonishing in their sweetness, and some whose boldness reminds us that Scheffler is still a mystical poet, even though he intended this work for popular appeal. Let us look more closely at some of the individual poems.

II *Advent*

Book I begins with a series of poems of yearning, some of which are demonstrably dependent upon love songs. The erotic quality of these poems is restrained somewhat by the occasional reminder that Jesus is an infant. However, this permits, on the one hand, what the modern reader is likely to sense as a trivialization of God in the little baby Jesus and, on the other, a direct descent into what even in the context of the seventeenth century must be called *Kitsch* when the infant Jesus is compared with the god Amor (I, xvii, stanza 1). Furthermore, this assumption can sometimes lead to startling images that one would be more likely to find in the work of a female poet:

> Wart' ich wil auff die Höhen
> Deß Myrrhen-Bergs gehen/
> Daß ich dich Myrren-Püschlein, find':
> Und wenn ich dich funden
> Verwundt und gebunden/
> So wil ich dich legen/
> Um deiner zu pflegen/
> Wo meine beyde Brüste sind (I, iv, stanza 9).

> (Wait, I will go to the heights
> Of the mountain of myrrh,
> So that I may find you, dear myrrh-bush.
> And when I have found you,
> Wounded and bound,
> Then I will lay you down
> To care for you
> Where my two breasts are.)

Apart from the bonds and the wounds, which are a prefiguration of the Passion (and do not belong thematically to this part of the series), there is here a clear recollection of the Song of Songs;

and this reminiscence comes through very strongly at many places in Book I. It is not so much a matter of verbal echoes, although there are some, but rather of the highly charged atmosphere and the richness of sensual metaphor, as well as the movement of wandering and search which characterizes the structure of the Biblical book:

> Sag mir ob ich beyn F[l]üssen
> Soll deiner geniessen/
> Weil du der starcke Liebs-Strom bist?
> Sag ob wir beyn Flammen
> Solln kommen zusammen?
> Daß du mich durchglüest/
> Mein Hertze besihest/
> Obs lauter in dich schmeltzt und fliesst.
>
> Nun wil ich mich außrüsten/
> Durchwandern die Wüsten
> Umb dich mein Turtel-Täubelein:
> Ich will mich bemühen
> Sehr ferne zu ziehen:
> Kein Ungemach achten/
> Nur embsiglich trachten/
> Wie daß ich möge bey dir seyn (I, iv, stanzas 4 and 5).
>
> (Tell me whether I shall
> Enjoy you by the rivers
> Because you are the strong stream of love?
> Say whether we shall
> Come together by the flames
> So that you may inflame me,
> Look upon my heart
> To see whether it melts and flows purely in you.
>
> Now I will outfit myself
> And wander through the wastelands
> For your sake, my turtle-dove.
> I will try
> To travel very far,
> Take notice of no hardship,
> Only strive diligently
> To discover how I may be with you.)

Stanzas such as these occur everywhere in the *Holy Joy of the Soul,* especially in the first book.

There seems to be literally nothing which Scheffler cannot turn to his account metaphorically, whether the images are drawn out of the erotic realm or from the complex of the Christ story itself. In an image which was to have much prominence in Pietism, Psyche regards her heart as the crêche in which Jesus is to be born (I, xiii) and distributes gifts in the role of the Three Wise Men (I, xx, stanza 6). A favorite rhetorical device of the seventeenth century occurs frequently: lines which begin with the same words (anaphora) continue in a succession of metaphor which attempts to capture the object in a net of language. In I, xxi, this device forms a sort of litany in which every first and third line begins with the words *Sei gegrüßt* ("Hail"), followed by a rich succession of metaphors, such as " . . . you true light, star which never loses its brilliance" (stanza 3); " . . . you thousand-times beautiful lily-white Nazarene" (stanza 4); " . . . you oil of Balsam, medicine of my sick soul" (stanza 6); and so on through eight stanzas. Coupled with this hyperbolic extravagance, however, there is a lively awareness, proper to the mystic, that in fact such comparisons are weak and inadequate, that language in fact cannot form a fine enough net to capture the transcendental magnificence of the Son of God. Scheffler adumbrates this perception in one of the really outstanding poems of the *Holy Joy of the Soul,* I, xxx, which is entitled "She Does Not Know with What She Shall Compare the Beauty of the Child Jesus," and begins:

> Du allerschönstes Bild wem soll ich dich vergleichen?
> Den weissen Lilien? Dem bundten Tausend-schön?
> Dem Zucker-Röselein? Ach nein: denn sie vergehn/
> Verdorren und verbleichen.

> (You most lovely image, with what shall I compare you?
> The white lilies? The colorful daisy?
> The sugar-rose? Oh, no, for they pass away,
> Wither and grow pale.)

At the same time that the poet demonstrates his range and skill of imagery, its insufficiency is stressed because it belongs to an incongruent mode of being. The flowers are transitory and thus completely inadequate in the realm of the eternal. The short, sober fourth line, with which each of the five stanzas ends, effectively denies the familiar abundance of the long Alexandrine lines; and indeed the poem ends with the assertion "Drum ist es besser schweigen" ("Therefore it is better to be silent"). This is in fact the same fruitful paradox which informs the *Cherubinic Wanderer:* by esthetic means the poet rouses the attention of the reader and gives it an impetus toward a goal which the esthetic element itself cannot reach. There is no Romanticism here, no notion that essential truth can be revealed *within* the realm of beauty. Nevertheless, the paradox here as elsewhere has its complications. Substantially, in a poem such as this the poet's value judgments must remain esthetically ordered even if the *implication* points to the transcendental realm:

> Vielleichte gleichst du dich dem Blitz der Seraphinē?
> Dem Thronen-Könige? Dem schönsten Engelein?
> Dem Cherubiner-Fürst? Ach nein es kan nicht seyn.
> Sie müssen dich bedienen (stanza 4).

> (Perhaps you are to be compared to the flash of the Seraphim?
> To the Thrones? to the prettiest angels?
> To the prince of the Cherubim? Oh no, it cannot be,
> They must serve you.)

Here the rank of Jesus in relation to the angelic hosts is tied firmly to esthetic rank. The inferiority of the angels implies *eo ipso* an incomparable inferiority in beauty. This predication of beauty as the appropriate value to the poetic context appears most clearly in a less attractive poem, I, xxxvii, "She Praises His Beauty," which begins:

> Schönster für dem sich neiget
> Alles was die Schönheit ehrt/
> Dem sich dienstbarlich erzeiget
> Was dem Himmel zugehört/
> Deine Liebe reitzet mich,
> Abermals zu loben dich/
> Daß ich muß die Saiten zwingen/
> Und von deiner Schönheit singen.

(Most beautiful one, before whom bows
Everything which honors beauty,
To whom servitude is rendered
By whatever belongs to Heaven,
Your love excites me
To praise you once again,
So that I must urge the strings
To sing of your beauty.)

The connection between great beauty and complete superordina-
tion is clear enough, but in the course of the poem, as so often in
the *Holy Joy of the Soul,* the vision becomes purely sensual:

Deine tausend-schönen Wangen
Sind zwei edler Hügelein/
Da mans Morgen-roth siht prangen
Bei dem frühen Tages-Schein.
Seynd zwey Felder derer Zier
Unverwelckt bleibt für und für:
Seynd zwey Berge da die Flammen
Und der Schnee bestehn beysammen (stanza 5).

(Your thousand-times beautiful cheeks
Are two noble hills
Where one sees the dawn glow
At the early light of day.
They are two fields whose charm
Remains unwithered forever,
Two mountains where the flames
And the snow endure side by side.)

And so on through thirteen stanzas.

The *Holy Joy of the Soul* astonishes the reader with its sheer
technical virtuosity. Although there are stretches where the poetic
intensity is not very great, and a good many forced rhymes and
the like do occur, such weaknesses are almost inevitable in a work
of this nature and are balanced by what for Scheffler's time is a
striking absence of technically bad lines or fumbled meters. A
rhythmically muddled line such as II, xliii, l.30 ("Wenn ér GOtt
sélbst so léiden síeht") is conspicuously rare. Scheffler, who despite his allegiance to Christian virtues shared the disdain of most

educated men of his time for the unlearned, strove in the *Holy Joy of the Soul* to keep the intellectual and poetic level down to that of the common folk. Nevertheless his poetic instincts led him to exploit the resources then available to verse to the fullest. An example is xxiii in the first book, entitled "She Rejoices Over the Birth of Christ":

> Jetz wird die Welt recht neu geborn/
> Jetz ist die Mayen-Zeit;
> Jetz thauet auff was war erfrorn/
> Und durch den Fall verschneyt!
> Jetz sausen die Winde
> Erquicklich und linde/
> Jetz singen die Lüffte/
> Jetz thönen die Grüffte/
> Jetz hüpfft und springet Berg und Thal (stanza 1).

> (Now the world is indeed newborn,
> Now is the May.
> Now what was frozen thaws out,
> And what was snowed in by the Fall [of Man].
> Now the winds blow
> Refreshing and mild;
> Now the breezes sing,
> Now the caves resound,
> Now mountain and valley hop and leap.)

With great deliberateness Scheffler predicates images of the springtime to the joy of Christmas, simultaneously transfiguring the event of the dead of winter and removing from the nature imagery its intrinsic autonomous character. In the last line of this stanza Scheffler demonstrates, once again, his instinct for the poetically dramatic passages of the Bible; for the astonishing image is surely a reminiscence of the beautiful little 114th Psalm and its famous fourth verse: "The mountains skipped [the Hebrew means literally 'danced'] like rams, the hills like young sheep." In every one of the five stanzas, seven out of the nine lines begin with the word *Jetz;* and this persistent anaphora threatens the poem with monotony. The threat is met by a simple rhythmic variation. The first four lines and the last line are composed in that iambic meter into which German, like English, so naturally falls; but the short lines five through eight are dactylic[10] and give a cheerful brightness to the tone which is eminently suitable to the sense of the verses. It is not known how seriously Scheffler thought about poetics as such, but the expansion and release he achieves in many places in the *Holy Joy of the Soul* by the introduction of three-syllable feet (which Opitz thought unsuitable for German poetry)[11] reminds one of the lighter, and, to be sure, more secular tone which the exploitation of dactyls and anapaests gave to German poetry in the latter part of the century.

Scheffler's effort to write simply and possibly also to create a Catholic counterpart to the immensely effective Protestant hymn, from time to time achieves a lyrical result that transcends the rather limited significance of the words themselves in a disciplined sureness of expression which is not typical of the period as a whole but reminds one not a little of the gifts of the master lyric poet of the age, Paul Fleming (1609–40). One almost perfect example of this kind is I, xxiv, where with severely limited means of form and content Scheffler has accomplished a poem which seems to beg for song. Here are the last two of the four stanzas:

> Es bringt uns alls mit sich
> Was wir wüntschen können/
> Heilt den alten Schlangen-Stich
> Und die krancken Sinnen:
> Singet diesem Kindelein/
> Lieblichs JEsulein/
> Laß mich gentz dein eigen seyn/
> Lieblichs JEsulein.
>
> Es macht uns GOtt zum Freund/
> Wil uns von dem bösen/
> Welcher uns zu stürtzen meynt/
> Ewiglich erlösen:
> Singet diesem Kindelein/
> Lieblichs JEsulein,
> Laß mich gantz dein eigen seyn/
> Lieblichs JEsulein.
>
> (He brings us everything with him
> That we could wish,
> Heals the old serpent bite

And the sick senses.
Sing to this little child,
Dear little Jesus,
Let me be completely your own,
Dear little Jesus

He makes God our friend,
Wants to redeem us
Eternally from the evil
Which thinks to overthrow us.
Sing to this little child [*etc.*]))

What may read as saccharine and trivial in English is dissolved in the German lyric in a genuine and even poignant sweetness. It is unfortunate that Scheffler, with his frequent infelicity in his titles, provided these fine verses with the dreadful heading, "She Sings of the Usefulness of His Birth."

Space is lacking to discuss Scheffler's wide range of stanza forms in detail. They range from four to nine lines, with four- and eight-line stanzas predominating, as is natural in a work meant to be set to music. The rhyme schemes occur in a variety of combinations; and there are frequent artful variations in line length, of which an example is the following first stanza of I, xxxix, which is remarkable in other respects as well:

Jesu du mächtiger Liebes-Gott
    Nah dich zu mir:
Denn ich verschmachte fast biß in Tod
    Für Liebs-Begier:
Ergreiff die Waffen/ und in Eil
Durchstich mein Hertz mit deinem Pfeil/
    Verwunde mich/
    [Verwunde mich].

(Jesus, you mighty god of love,
    Come close to me,
For I am languishing nearly to death
    From desire for love.
Take up your weapons and with haste
Stab my heart with your arrow,
    Wound me,
    Wound me.)

An example of the outer boundary of Scheffler's formal experimentation is I, xxxiii, a poem of a type which Opitz called "Echo," [12] where the last words of a line are either answered in a single rhyme or simply repeated, a form particularly suitable to this poem, which is a catechism on the love of God:

Wer wird mir mein Hertze das Jesulein geben?
    Heiliges Leben.
Wo werd' ichs berührē mit Armen und Lippen?
    Gehe zur Krippen.
Was Krippe? So liegt deñ der König im Stalle?
    Ach ja im Stalle! (stanza 1).

(Who, my heart, will give me the little Jesus?
    A holy life.
Where will I touch him with arms and lips?
    Go to the manger!
What, manger? Does the King then lie in the stable?
    Ah, yes, in the stable!

III *Passion and Resurrection*

All the above examples have been taken from the first book and could be multiplied without difficulty by verses from the other four, although it seems most appropriate to regard the first three books as one unit, the fourth as another, and the fifth as a third. (It should be noted that although the work is divided into books, the poems are numbered consecutively from beginning to end.) The danger of overplaying the erotic imagery is present intermittently throughout the first three books and is enhanced by the ubiquitous model of the Song of Songs. A poem such as II, lii, entitled, "Psyche Desires to Be a Bee on the Wounds of Jesus," will in the psychologically trained mind of the modern reader call up associations that may not necessarily be religious. The famous opening verse of the forty-second Psalm, "As the hart panteth after the water brooks, so panteth my soul after Thee, O God," is turned to similar account in II, lv:

Wie ein Hirsch zur dürren Zeit
Nach dem frischen Wasser schreyt,
Also schreyet auch mit Schmertzen
Nach dem Wasser deines Hertzen/

JEsu meine matte Seel
In der dürren Leibes-Höl (stanza 1).

(As a hart in time of drought
Cries out for fresh water,
So, Jesus, also cries with pain
For the water of your heart
My faint soul
In its dry body-cave.) [13]

In the outburst of joy at the Resurrection in the third book, and
the subsequent emotion of longing which reasserts itself after the
Ascension, the erotic motif reappears. Psyche refers to Jesus as her
beloved shepherd in a poem which must have a secular model
(III, lxviii), although none has been found; and the second stanza
of the following poem contains a parody of genuine seduction:

Die Sonne hat sich schon gesenckt/
Die Nacht ist da/ die mich bedrengt;
Kom doch herein/ mein Freuden-Schein/
Zünd' an mein Hertz wie eine Kertz/
Erleucht' es gantz mit deinem Glantz/
Daß ich dich mög erkennen/
Und durch und durch entbrennen (III, lxix, stanza 2).

(The sun has already set,
The night which oppresses me is here.
Oh come inside, my gleam of joy,
Light my heart like a candle,
Illuminate it all with your glory,
So that I may recognize you
And burn up through and through.)

After Jesus' ascent into Heaven, the seventh stanza of III, lxxv, is
also a parody of erotic remembrance:

Liebkost mich jetzt nicht seine Huld/
So ist er meines Todes Schuld/
Dieweil er selbst offt früh und spat
Zur Liebe mich gereitzet hat.

(If his favor does not caress me now,
Then he will be guilty of my death,

> Because he himself often early and late
> Excited me to love.)

Psyche is drawn after him no matter how he flees (III, lxxxi),
longs to kiss him on the mouth (III, lxxxiv; lxxxv), and even his
odor arouses her "eternal desire of love" (III, lxxxvii). How risky
this precedure can become is shown by the twelfth stanza of III,
ciii, a poem, incidentally, that contains over fifty sensual images
for Jesus and Psyche's love for him:

> Ich frage nu wenig mehr nach dem Himmel/
> Nach Edens Lust und Welt-Getümmel;
> Du bist mir eine gantze Welt;
> Du bist der Himmel/ den ich meyne;
> Das Paradeiß/ das mir alleine
> Für allen andern wolgefällt.

> (Now I ask very little after Heaven any more,
> After Eden's joy and worldly tumult;
> You are for me a whole world.
> You are the Heaven that I mean,
> The Paradise that pleases me alone
> Beyond all other things.)

One wonders upon reading this stanza—the sense of which, incidentally, is not entirely clear—whether Scheffler has been seduced
by some popular model or whether he has lost track of his intentions. For to keep the statement from being pure heresy would
require a subtle mystical interpretation of a kind which is not
otherwise appropriate to the poems of this popular *vademecum*.

The second book begins with a contemplation of the Passion,
opening with a vision of Gethsemane (xli) and a description of
the scourging in a lament which exploits the familiarity of the age
with scenes of brutality (xlii). The following poem describes the
carrying of the Cross in a rough trochaic rhythm which gives a
peculiar marching sound. The last line of each stanza reverts to
iambs, creating a more comtemplative contrast:

> Schauet, wie er geht gebücket/
> Wie das Creutz jhn nieder drücket!
> Schauet wie er ist verstellet/

Wie er auff die Erden fället/
Für übergrosser Mattigkeit! (II, xliii, stanza 5).

(See how he walks bowed down,
How the Cross weighs him down!
See how he is disfigured,
How he falls upon the ground
From too much weariness!)

The next group of poems describes the details of the Crucifixion, with individual attention to Jesus' battered face (xlv), his wounds (xlvi)—expanded in the tenth stanza to a whole metaphorical landscape of suffering—his feet (xlvii), and his arms and hands (xlviii). The latter poem contains a rare direct homily in the form of a prayer:

Gib daß ich nicht müde werde
Guts zu thun auff dieser Erde
Mit meinen Händen was ich kann:
Daß ich deine Leiden preise/
Und dir wieder Dienst erweise/
Weil du hast mir so viel gethan (stanza 7.)

(Grant that I do not grow tired
Of doing good on this earth
With my hands as well as I can;
That I praise your sufferings
And return you service
Because you have done so much for me.)

The series goes on to describe his eyes (xlix), his Crown of Thorns (l), and the Sacred Heart (li). The ecstatic quality of these meditations grows steadily through these and the following poems, until in II, li, Psyche begs agonizedly for admission to the Sacred Heart and in the following poem, mentioned above, desires to be a bee on the wounds of Jesus. Poem lvi, "Her Love is Crucified," opens a series of laments at the death of Jesus, but, with an eye to theological considerations, the tone is on the whole restrained, and the poems are not allowed to end on a note of despair. Poem lx, in fact, expresses suitable gratitude for the death of Jesus, and in lxi Psyche prays for a similarly blessed end. In the

penultimate poem of Book II (lxiii), Psyche seats herself under
the Cross and expands the event to universal relevance:

> Kommet her jhr allesam
> Die jhr schwach und abgemattet;
> Setzt euch unter diesen Stamm/
> Daß er eure Seel beschattet:
> Eilt dem heilgen Creutze zu/
> Denn jhr findt da wahre Ruh (stanza 5).

> (Come here, all of you
> Who are weak and worn out,
> Seat yourselves under this trunk
> That it may shade your soul.
> Hurry to the sacred Cross,
> For there you will find true peace.)

The third book begins with an abrupt contrast to the elegiac
mood of the Passion and the following prayers; for the Resurrection brings an outburst of joy in a poem of complex rhythms,
which reminds one strongly of the secular pastoral poetry of the
age:

> Nun ist dem Feind zerstöret seine Macht/
>   Der Tod ist todt/
> Und uns das Leben wiederbracht!
>   Singet und klingt/
>   Hüpffet und springt/
>   Jubilirt/
> Unser JEsus triumphirt (lxv, stanza 1).

> (Now the might of the Adversary is destroyed,
>   Death is dead,
> And life brought back to us.
>   Sing and sound,
>   Hop and leap,
>   Exult,
> Our Jesus triumphs.)

This outburst of joy is disciplined immediately in the following
piece (lxvi), "She Describes the Magnificence of His Resurrection," a poem strictly in the sober manner of the traditional Prot-

estant hymn. The Resurrection and Ascension, however, bring the disappearance of Jesus from the immediate scene; and the longing for the absent Jesus gives the occasion for the return of the persistent erotic metaphor discussed above. Gradually, Scheffler turns the attention of the reader to other matters, such as the Eucharist ("You sugar-sweet bread of Heaven," xci, 1.1; see also xcvii). Psyche prays to Mary, the angels, the fathers, the Apostles, the Martyrs, and the Virgins to lend her their qualities in order to make her worthy of the Bridegroom (xcvi), Psyche prays to become like them:

> Oder wär ich wie Narcissen
> Bey den stillen Wasser-Flüssen!
> Oder wie ein Hyacinth/
> Den man himmel-farben findt!
> Nnd wie niedrige Violn/
> Die man muß im Grase holn (civ, stanza 5).

> (Or were I like narcissus
> By the still rivers,
> Or like a hyacinth
> Which is found the color of Heaven,
> And like lowly violets,
> Which must be picked in the grass.)

Once more reminiscences from the Song of Songs are very much in evidence:

> Oder wär ich wie ein Garten
> Voll Gewürtze bester Arten!
> Daß mein JEsus für und für
> Sich ergetzen könt' in mir/
> Und mit Lust stäts bey mir seyn,
> Wie in einem ewgen Mayn (civ, stanza 6).

> (Or if I were like a garden
> Full of the best spices!
> So that my Jesus forever
> Could enjoy himself in me
> And be with me always with pleasure
> As in an eternal May.)

To bring the pattern of the liturgical year to a close, Psyche comes finally upon the scene of the Nativity and engages in a dialogue with the shepherds and the Christ child, which contains, incidentally, a daring parody of a drinking song:

> *Die Hirten*
> Kom̃t/ wir wollen alle trincken/
> Biß wir werden truncken seyn/
> Biß wir gantz und gar versincken
> In dem Quall und in dem Wein;
> Biß uns Red' und Wort gebricht/
> Und sich keiner kennet nicht (III, cvi, stanza 12).

> (*The Shepherds*
> Come, we all will drink
> Until we shall be drunk,
> Until we sink completely
> In the well and in the wine,
> Until we lose our speech
> And none knows himself.)

The third book ends with a series of hymns of praise (cxviii–cxxii) and a final dissolution into the substance of God (cxxiii).

IV   *Recapitulation*

Since books I–III have an obviously closed structure, and the fourth book was published separately, although also in 1657, it is doubtful whether the latter was written in conjunction with the first three. It is in fact impossible to detect any principle of structural ordering in Book IV, which contains thirty-two poems on a wide variety of subjects. It begins with a poem in praise of the Virgin Mary, which is curiously slack (cxxiv), and goes on to the figures of John the Evangelist (cxxv) and Mary Magdalene ("You sweet friend of my Lord," cxxvi, 1.5) This leads Psyche to an act of contrition in her own right (cxxvii), exclusively concentrated in the degree of her love of Jesus: her sense of sin is relieved not by repentance, but by recognition of Christ's sacrifice. Shortly thereafter appears a poem in which Psyche renounces her desire for all things, including the beauties of creation (cxxxix); and in the love poems which follow (cxxx-cxxxvii) the agonized yearning of books I and III is replaced by a new certainty of the possession of Jesus' love. Indeed, Jesus engages himself to her, and it is now he who is described as in love (cxxxii). At this point any trace of order vanishes. There is a poem about the Nativity (cxxxviii) and one about the baby Jesus (cxxxix), followed by two Crucifixion scenes (cxl–cxli), the first of which is the only poem in the *Holy Joy of the Soul* written entirely in Alexandrines. These are followed by five poems (cxlii–cxlvi) in which the nightingale and the phenomena of spring are used in urgent praise of Jesus. The remaining poems, which may be described generally as hymns, contain here and there some new elements. Particularly interesting is the fourth stanza of III, cxlviii:

> Es lobe dich HERR mein Verstand und Wille/
> GOtt mein Gedächtnüß lobe dich:
> Zu deinem Lob sey meine Bildung stille/
> Mein Geist erheb sich über sich:
> Mein Athem lob dich für und für/
> Mein Puls schlag stäts das Sanctus dir:
> Es singen alle meine Glieder
> Zu deinen Ehren tausend Lieder.

> (May my understanding and my will praise Thee, Lord,
> My memory praise Thee, God;
> To Thy praise let my learning be still,
> My spirit rise above itself.
> May my breath praise Thee forever,
> My pulse always beat the Sanctus.
> All my limbs sing
> A thousand songs to Thy praise.)

The first four lines of this stanza, in which the qualities of mind are harnessed and subdued to the transcendental purpose, introduce mystical material otherwise quite infrequent in the *Holy Joy of the Soul*. The reference to *Bildung*—learning or education—indicates another tension in Scheffler, that between the pride of the learned, which he shared with the intellectual world of his time, and its religious subordination to the unaffected service of God.

Another poem (cliv), entitled, "She Prays for the Friends of her Beloved," is one of the rare occasions where Scheffler's vision, at least in his major poetic period, expands to include in the New

Covenant anyone other than himself. The book ends on a somber note, however. The final poem (clv), entitled, "Consideration of Painful Eternity," begins darkly:

> O Ewigkeit! O Ewigkeit!
> Mein Hertz muß in mir weinen/
> Wenn es das Unend deiner Zeit
> Bedenckt und deine Peinen:
> Ich werde blaß und ungestalt
> Ob deiner Jahre Länge:
> Ich bin erstaunt und sterbe bald
> Für deiner Qualen Menge!
> Ach/ ach was ist die Ewigkeit (stanza 1).

> (O Eternity! O Eternity!
> My heart must weep within me
> When it considers the endlessness
> Of your time and your pain.
> I become pale and shapeless
> On account of the length of your years.
> I am amazed and shall soon die
> Before the quantity of your torments.
> Oh, oh, what is eternity!)

The grim tone of this long poem of thirteen stanzas reminds one forcibly of Gryphius and, even more strongly, of the mighty and famous Protestant hymn of Johann Rist, *O Ewigkeit du Donnerwort* (also 1657), without, however, attaining the quality of either.

V   *Unsuccessful Self-Imitation*

Book V, published eleven years afterwards in the second edition of the *Holy Joy of the Soul* in 1668, is one of Scheffler's weakest works. Although many of the themes and motifs of the first four books are picked up again, the poetic intensity has, for the most part, fallen off sharply, and the diction has become more conventional. There are many fewer moments of poetic excitement than in any of the preceding books. In this book it is clear that intent has won the victory over vision. The specifically Catholic tendency of the work as a public tract has come to the foreground. This appears at the very beginning in a poem in praise of the

Immaculate Conception that, despite its promising structure of sections corresponding to the daily services, is trivial and uninteresting. The strongly liturgical quality of Book V is apparent in a prayer for chastity (clix); a grace for meals (clxii); a vesper-song (clxiii); three poems in praise of the Holy Ghost (clxxxviii–cxc), the first two of which appear to be versions of Latin hymns; a learnedly theological praise of the Trinity (cxci); poems on the Eucharist (cxcii, cxciii); and hymns to Mary (cciii, cciv). New, however, is a prayer for a blessing on the author's poetry (clx, l.49). Two poems (cxcvii, cxcviii), the second of which contains a thinly veiled polemic in reference to the role of Peter, praise God for the preservation of the Church. Probably the spiritual nadir is reached in a poem entitled "The Crown of Eternal Salvation" (ccii), which despite its aspirations is crippled by an overabundance of worldly metaphor which binds the vision to earthly vanities.

In the midst of these are found some poems which pick up the theme of erotic longing as it is found in Books I and III (clxiv–clxviii, clxxiv, clxxix–clxxxv). But although the sensuality of the earlier poems is not entirely absent, the tone is paler and much more cautious. It is as though the forty-three-year-old ascetic had lost even the memory of those passions which in his thirties he had channeled into a religious direction. Like the other poems of Book V, this group lacks the rhythmic and strophic imaginativeness which characterizes the early work. In one poem, Psyche appears as the sister rather than the lover of Jesus (clxxix); and in another, reflecting the certainty which began to appear in Book IV, Jesus hunts her as a deer (clxxxii), rather than the other way around, as in III, lxxxi. Only here and there are there traces of the old yielding intensity, as in the following stanza:

> Kom̃/ hier ist/ was du gesucht/
> Hier ist deiner Liebe Frucht;
> Kom̃/ hier magst du frey umbfangen/
> Deme du bist nachgegangen:
> Kom̃/ du treuer Schäfer du/
> Meiner Seele Trost und Ruh (V, clxxxiii, stanza 4).

> (Come, here is what you have sought,
> Here is the fruit of your love;

> Come, here you may freely embrace
> What you have gone after.
> Come, you true shepherd,
> The consolation and peace of my soul.)

Here one again suspects a secular model.

VI *Unexpected Virtues*

In spite of its occasional felicities, one is inclined to ignore Book V as a distinctly minor work. The same cannot be said, however, of the remainder of the *Holy Joy of the Soul,* to which a survey such as the foregoing cannot do full justice. Many as its defects may be, especially in the eyes of the modern reader, monotony is not one of them, which is all the more astonishing in view of the sharp limitations Scheffler placed upon the religious and intellectual range of the work. Even though the so-called *Jesusminne,* with its studied triviality, may be tiresome and even embarrassing as an expression of religious experience, one becomes increasingly attracted and charmed by the work as one reads it. There are two chief reasons for this. For one thing, the range of imagery and the inventiveness of form and metaphorical scene is extraordinarily wide. Although many of the poems are indifferent in and of themselves, rarely can it be said that one poem is so much like another as to give a feeling of superfluity. The fact that Scheffler consciously and purposefully drew upon a variety of models—secular poetry, Catholic and Protestant devotional literature, and, above all, the Song of Songs—does not detract from his achievement. This variety, coupled with the relative refinement and the control of language, contributes greatly to the attractiveness of the work. The second element is, paradoxically enough, in another sense one of the work's weaknesses. The sheer daring of the erotic imagery, which establishes a tension in the poetry, is not without its fascination; and it is difficult to believe that the author of the *Cherubinic Wanderer* was completely unaware of the excitement which this tightrope performance between devotion and lust often generates. All in all, the *Holy Joy of the Soul* makes one wonder what Scheffler might have achieved had he kept his mind and heart concentrated upon his poetic vocation.

CHAPTER 4

Unhappy End: Sensual Description of the Four Last Things

I *Unbearable Wilderness*

HANS LUDWIG HELD, one of the most thorough students of Scheffler's work and, judging from some passages in his writing, himself a devout Catholic, calls the *Sensual Description of the Four Last Things* of 1674 an "unbearable wilderness." [1] Indeed, no one but Scheffler's most extreme Catholic defenders has ever had a good word to say about this work; and many readers have reacted to it with shock and horror. Even such an excited aversion, however, seems to the sober observer to do the poem more justice than it deserves. It is less atrocious than simply bad and unworthy of the author of the *Cherubinic Wanderer* and the *Holy Joy of the Soul*—the work of a man who no longer cares anything for poetry and is completely obsessed by his evangelistic purposes.

The *Sensual Description* consists of 309 stanzas of eight iambic lines, alternating four and three stresses, and rhymed *ababcdcd*. They are distributed unequally in four parts on the subjects of "Death" (20), "The Last Judgment" (60), "The Eternal Sufferings of the Damned" (72), and "The Eternal Joys of the Blessed" (157). The metrical pattern is never varied except for an occasional dactylic line; and so the work must be seen as a single four-part poem of 2,472 lines. That is a long poem; and it is subject to all the weaknesses that prevent any but a very few long poems in world literature from being successful: failure to sustain poetic tension, disunity in image and profile, and a descent into toilsomely rhymed prose. As is the case with the rest of Scheffler's poetic productions, it is not possible to say exactly when it was written. The imprint date is 1675, but is was published in 1674; and Ellinger suggests that it was composed in that year.[2] Clearly it is Scheffler's last known original poetic work, and one is very willing

to believe that it reflects his spiritual state as he was approaching the nadir of his tormented life.

Scheffler prefaced the *Sensual Description* with a bitter and
somewhat strange apology, which combines a sense of great weariness with a rather shamefaced defense of his method of present-
ing the terrors of Hell and the joys of Heaven in purely earthly
images. He begins by saying that men do not consider these
things sufficiently and that they regard the facts of their future as
a dream. With a clear swipe at the pseudo-Classical conventions
of much conventional poetry (including the appearance of Amor
in his own *Holy Joy of the Soul*), he asserts: "Because I am to
treat of such serious and true things, I have wished to refrain
completely from all and every name and story invented by the
pagans with which poets otherwise are accustomed to lard and
decorate their writings, so that I will give no one reason to regard
such things as fable or mere poetry. Which it indeed is not, but
the pure dry truth, for which I need no proof." [3] The renunciation
of pseudo-Classical tropes seems to go a step farther to a renunciation of poetry altogether. Indeed he speaks of his poem only as
"German rhymes." [4] He goes on to say that he is well aware that
the other world will be crystalline and that no gold and silver will
be found there. Nevertheless the Bible uses such symbols of pre-
ciousness to give at least an indication of the glories of Heaven;
and so the poet is justified in this process since a true description
of these things is beyond mortal powers anyway. All this seems
traditional enough and could no doubt stand unchallenged, were
it not for the strangely earth-bound manner in which Scheffler
expresses it. Whereas we are more likely to think of the Biblical
images as an attempt to give an inkling of glories which are quali-
tatively different from earthly glories, Scheffler seems to be talking about a quantitative difference: Heaven will contain jewels
and precious metals, merely more glorious than those we know.
But the full extent of the shrinkage of his religious imagination
appears when, in one of the most disastrous sentences he ever
wrote, he describes the joys of Heaven as an exact *quid pro quo*
for the deprivations of the Christian ascetic: "For, because the
eye, for the sake of God, has refrained from looking upon gay and
desirable things, the ear has turned away from hearing indecent
and vain talk, the taste has deprived itself of delicate foods, the

sense of smell has endured much stink among the sick and the poor, and the touch has borne much pain and harshness, so it is also proper that each sense will have its particular reward and pleasure." [5] The sentence reads almost as if the ascetic's ears will be rewarded with indecent and vain talk in Heaven. Rather weakly he assures us: " . . . to be sure, it will all be in a Heavenly and not an earthly manner." [6] All limitations and the ultimate triviality of the *Sensual Description* are manifest in these lines.

Once again Scheffler is working with models before him. Chief among them is the Bible itself, which Scheffler here follows more closely than in any other work, sometimes paraphrasing passages from the Gospels verse for verse. Furthermore, it is clear that a number of Jesuit songs stood godfather to a good many stanzas, at least in the first and second parts.[7] In fact, a footnote of Scheffler's indicates that he thought of the *Sensual Description* as a text to be sung and makes a suggestion as to how the immensely long fourth part might be divided into four sections for that purpose.[8] But despite the models of the Bible and the contemporary Jesuit verses, some of which are more sophisticated than Scheffler's own work, the literal vision is medieval in the worst sense of the word. Held argues that in Scheffler's time only a few isolated enlightened souls had escaped from literalness and superstition, whereas the majority of men still believed that "the rainbow . . . spanned Heaven and earth as a glowing bridge; the will-o'-wisp over the swamps was the weeping soul of a dead child; scaffold and Calvary were still the altar of the . . . Devil; the witch's terrible power of curse still existed as a frightening reality." [9] But 1675 is nevertheless a late date to excuse a poet and intellectual on such grounds, especially when he began his career in the vast imaginative reaches of mysticism. The *Sensual Description,* after all, appeared more than forty years after the Jesuit poet Spee had written his book against the witch trials.

II   *"Death"*

The first and shortest part of the work, "Death," has always been regarded as the least unattractive, perhaps not so much for its poetic quality, which is indifferent, as for the studied rejection

of one of the most annoying conventions of the Baroque age: the
idolizing adulation of highborn and highly placed persons.
Scheffler stresses that death is no respecter of persons and threatens with grim certainty even those who strive after "property and
high rank" (I, l.4). Furthermore, there are moments when
Scheffler comes as close as he ever does to sympathetic poignancy,
such as the description of fear at the last moment (stanza 7) and
the utter isolation of a man in the hour of his death:

> Die Freunde werden allzumal
> Von deinem Bette weichen
> Und sich verlieren aus dem Saal,
> In dem du wirst verbleichen (stanza 11, ll. 1–4).[10]

> (Your friends will all at once
> Depart from your bed
> And disappear from the room
> In which you will grow pale.)

In the tenth stanza Scheffler calls up the gnawing of conscience,
and in stanzas fifteen and sixteen he attacks the pride of men by
graphically describing the worms to which the buried corpse is
subject. The section ends with a general, and for the time, wholly
conventional reflection upon the transitoriness of all things (17,
18), and a hortatory homiletic urging men to repent (19, 20).

All this would be harmless and familiar if Scheffler did not seem
to be going out of his way, even in the first part, to concentrate his
frustrations and bitterness in a tone that is nothing short of dis-
tasteful. The very beginning of the work contains an irony the
ageing poet undoubtedly did not have the wit to perceive. To
each of the four parts Scheffler prefixed a Biblical motto; and for
"Death" he chose Psalm 39:5: "Lord, make me to know my end,
and the measure of my days, what it is; let me know how short-
lived I am." Then Scheffler begins his poem:

> Ihr dummen Sterblichen, die ihr
> So frei und sicher lebet . . .

> (You stupid mortals, who
> Live so freely and certainly . . .)

The juxtaposition of the lines could not be more incongruous. Unfair as it may ordinarily be to compare such verse with the glories of the Psalter, it was Scheffler who put the lines together; and he thereby reveals not only the contrast between the troubled humility of the psalm and his aggressive and arrogant attack, but also a complete insensitivity to poetic values.

III *"The Last Judgment"*

The second part of the poem is entitled "The Last Judgment," and its course is, on the whole, what one would expect, especially in view of its closeness to Biblical sources, which supply most of the imagery and excitement in what is unquestionably the most effective of the four parts. The motto is taken from II Peter 3:10: "But the day of the Lord will come like a thief, and then the heavens will pass away with a loud noise, and the elements will be dissolved with fire, and the earth and works that are upon it will be burned up." This is followed by the annunciation of the Day, with strong echoes from the *Dies irae* of the Mass, and a warning call to "princes, emperors, kings, . . . Lord and Potentates . . . , Pope and high clergy . . . , bishops and prelates . . . , judges" (stanza 2, ll. 1–5), following which the earth breaks open (stanzas 3–6) and is visited by fire and plagues (stanza 7). The trumpet calls the dead (stanza 8), who rise (stanzas 9–11) as the bloody Cross and the tools of the Passion appear (stanzas 12–14). The next two stanzas describe the fear of the risen and the vain wish for mortality:

> Dort schreit der: Wär ich nie geborn
> Noch je geschaffen worden!
> Wär ich im Mutterleib verlorn,
> Könnt ich mich selbst ermorden! (stanza 16, ll. 1–4).

> (There one cries: Would I had never been born
> Nor ever created!
> Would that I had been lost in my mother's womb,
> That I could murder myself!)

Christ appears as a judge with sword and lily (stanzas 17–19), as the angels divide the sheep from the goats (stanzas 20–21). The natural bonds between man and wife, father and son, friends, and

brother and sister are broken. Christ dispenses grace to the inno-
cent as a reward for their compassionate works (stanzas 23–26) in
a close paraphrase of Matt 25:34–40. The damnation begins with
the Roman persecutors of the Christians, Maximin, Hadrian,
Commodus, Nero, Severus, and Decius (stanzas 27–31), where-
upon Satan begins his accusation against the sinners through
eleven stanzas (34–44), in the course of which the Seven Deadly
Sins, hyperbolically described, are given a stanza each: pride
(35), covetousness (36), envy (37), anger (38), gluttony (39),
lust (40), and sloth (41). The poet derives all these sins from a
lack of love and hope:

> In Summa, es war keine Lieb
> In ihrer Brust zu finden,
> Noch Hoffnung, die deins Geistes Trieb
> Im Herzen pflegt zu gründen.
> Bei vielen war der Glaub allein
> Und doch nur in dem Munde,
> Ihr ganzes Leben war ein Schein,
> Kein Wesen in dem Grunde (stanza 42).

> (In sum, there was no love
> To be found in their breast,
> Nor hope which the force of Thy spirit
> Is wont to found in the heart [syntax is uncertain here].
> Many had faith alone,
> And yet only in their mouth;
> Their whole life was a pretense,
> No essence at the bottom.)

The reference to "faith alone" is of course an unsubtle swipe at the
Lutherans. After Satan delivers his peroration, Christ awaits the
sinners' defense, but they have none to give (stanza 45). He turns
to the Saints to ask whether there can be any forgiveness (stanza
46; but they self-righteously deny it because they, for their part,
succeeded in overcoming the temptations to which the accused
have succumbed (stanzas 47–50). Similarly to the salvation of the
blessed, the condemnation (stanzas 51–59) also paraphrases Matthew (25:41–46). Stanza 60 tersely describes the descent into Hell
and the ascension of the blessed.

IV *Hellfire and Brimstone*

It is the third section, "The Eternal Torments of the Damned,"
that has generally aroused the horror of the critics because of the
sadistic violence of its description, which was prefigured, incidentally, many years earlier in three of the sonnets in the *Cherubinic
Wanderer* (VI, 5, 6, 7). Men of our own time, who have witnessed man-made horrors on a scale undreamed of even by that
terrorized age, are less likely than critics of the more genteel nineteenth century to flinch at Scheffler's all but insane visions. Moreover, Ellinger is probably right when he remarks that "Scheffler
was speaking to a generation whose nerves were dulled by the
atrocities of war, the torments of torture, and public executions." [11]
Certainly it cannot be said that Scheffler's phantasmagoria is any
ghastlier than Dante's. What differentiates it is precisely the lack
of that quality which makes Dante's *Inferno* endlessly gripping
despite its sequence of horrors: the Italian poet's inextinguishable
fascination for and interest in the individual personalities of the
damned. There are no persons in Scheffler's Hell, only nameless
sinners exposed to excruciating torments without any regard to
their humanity.

The third part begins with a lament upon the enormity of eternity, which again has echoes of Rist's *O Ewigkeit du Donnerwort*
(see above, p. 123), a theme which recurs strongly toward the
end of this section (stanzas 61, 66, 71). The poet proceeds to an
observation upon the forgetfulness of men in this life (stanzas
2–4), and the rude awakening which awaits them (stanza 5).
Then Scheffler turns loose his cascade of torments: the damned
are seen as dogs (stanza 10) subjected to hellhounds (stanza 6),
chains (stanza 7), heat, cold, fire, and brimstone (stanzas 8–9),
molten lead (stanza 11), plague (stanza 12), vermin (stanza 13,
and snakes (stanzas 14–16). Because of their laziness of spirit in
this life, the damned are held immovable (stanzas 17–19) and are
tortured by birds of prey (stanza 21). Dr. Scheffler does not ne-
glect to mention that no medical relief is available for them
(stanza 22)—the stink is the relief they deserve, he remarks
(stanza 24). The hunger and thirst of the damned are satisfied
only by foul substances which Satan grants when he is a good
mood (stanza 25). They are subjected to excruciating noises

(stanzas 26–27) and, as though in a nightmare, can make no sound themselves (stanzas 28–29). Scheffler cannot refrain from interrupting at this point with verses of gleeful scorn:

> Schaut, die soll eure Kurzweil sein,
> Ihr schändlichen Schandierer!
> Dies sind die Hurenliedelein,
> Ihr Buhler, ihr Verführer! (stanza 31, ll. 1–4).

> (Look, this shall be your amusement,
> You shameful defilers!
> These are your whore-ditties,
> You gallants, you seducers!)

In the following seven stanzas (32–36) Scheffler concentrates on disfigurement of the body, whereby he reaches a level of barbarity hardly matched in literature:

> Dem hängt die Nase bis ins Maul,
> Der hat durchfreßne Backen,
> Dem dritten sind die Lippen faul,
> Dem vierten schwürt der Nacken.
> Ein anderer hat einen Kropf
> Wie eine Wasserkanne,
> Ein anderer glüht um den Kopf
> Wie indiansche Hanne (stanza 33).

> (This one's nose hangs into his mouth,
> The other has his cheeks eaten through,
> The third has rotting lips,
> The fourth's neck is abscessed.
> Another has a goitre
> Like a water-pitcher,
> Another glows red around his head
> Like Indian cocks.)

In addition to all this, the damned turn upon and torment one another (stanza 37), and are in turn tortured by devils (stanzas 39–47). Here another low point of sadism is reached:

> Den henkert man, wie man nur kann
> Den jaget man durch Spieße,

Den speiet man mit Feuer an,
Verhauet dem die Füße.
Die tritt man in den höllschen Kot,
Die schläget man mit Keulen,
Die nagelt man zu Hohn und Spott
Auf Stangen wie die Eulen (stanza 43).

(This one they hang as much as ever they can,
This one they chase with spears,
This one they spit fire upon,
Chop off this one's feet.
These are stamped into the Hellish filth,
These are beaten with clubs,
These are nailed to contempt and scorn
Like owls upon poles.)

And so on, stanza upon stanza.

In need now of a structural element to somehow harness this runaway chaos, Scheffler again turns to the Seven Deadly Sins and awards them appropriate punishments: Pride must kiss Satan's rear (stanza 49); Covetousness collects filth while molten gold is poured into his throat (stanzas 50–51); Envy eats his own heart (stanza 52); Gluttony has his excess substances torn out of him and must eat filth and drink pus (stanzas 53–54); Anger must bear the Devil's fury (stanza 55); Sloth is driven endlessly about (stanza 56); the lustful suffer intense pain (stanza 57); and the homosexuals are whipped with scorpions (stanza 58). Finally this madness grinds to a halt. After a summation (stanza 59), Scheffler reverts to the suffering knowledge of eternity (stanzas 60–63) in which the damned are exiled from God and vainly attempt either repentance or rebellion. Though they repent their lost salvation (stanzas 64–66), there is no escape from the worm that never dies (stanza 67). Now, snarls the poet, go ahead and sin (stanza 68). The final four stanzas contain a plea for repentance (69–72). That any man literate enough and patient enough to read these incredible 576 lines was ever brought to repentance by them may well be doubted.

V *Paradise*

The 157 stanzas of "The Eternal Joys of the Blessed" constitute over one half of the whole poem, and much of it is so dreary that it will not bear detailed discussion. The chief characteristic of this section is the peculiarity in the preface noted above: the description of Paradise as a riot of material, sensual pleasures offered as a reward for the earthly privations of the blessed and bordering, at least in one place (stanzas 141–42), on the swinish. It is a theology not of abandoning sensual things for higher things, but of abandoning them on earth in order to have them in the beyond—a theology of postponement. Despite Scheffler's attempt to turn the meal in Paradise (stanzas 133–42) into an allegory in which Christ serves his innocence, youth, wisdom, work, and obedience, the sugar of his love, the clarity of his soul, and the wine of the Holy Ghost, the total impression remains ineradicable. The first thirteen stanzas, with their description of pearly gates, streets paved with gold, alabaster houses with crystal windows and tapestried rooms, are a hyperbolic description of aristocratic palatial magnificence and nothing more. Surprising, however, is the description of the Heavenly gardens in the long passage extending from stanza 14 to stanza 38.

Nature is not a prominent element in Scheffler's poetry. From the day when he wrote *mundus pulcherrimum nihil,* his eye was turned resolutely away from terrestrial beauty. Such nature images that do occur are for the most part of the painted, conventional kind familiar from pastoral poetry. But there was obviously another side to the man. The sublimated eroticism of the *Holy Joy of the Soul,* the gross crudities of the third part of the *Sensual Description,* and the palpable pleasures of Paradise in the fourth part all suggest that his sensual receptivity had been roughly suppressed rather than allowed to mortify quietly. Here, suddenly, in the safety of his vision of Paradise, there are flowers, fruit trees, open fields, charming birds, and tame game, and, with what one would wish were a touch of humor but probably is not, sheep bearing silk instead of wool (stanza 29). It is an Arcadia without winter or bad weather, where rain and snow are on call for the pleasure of the inhabitants. The striking thing about the passage is its length; surely some mistrusted but persistent element in Scheffler's personality is here given free rein for the first time. Although in poetic quality the passage is not to be numbered among the great nature poems of Germany, it is like a ray of sunshine in this otherwise bleak work.

The angels and the blessed in glory are described as they pre-
pare for the great centerpiece of the section, the Heavenly banquet. There is a trace of mystical doctrine in the assertion, in
Stanza 53, that the blessed no longer need faith or mysteries because they now see everything clearly with full understanding.
The first two stanzas are an echo of the paradoxical expressions of
the poet's younger days:

> Sie dürfen die Dreifaltigkeit
> Nicht mehr im Glauben ehren . . .
>
> (They may no longer honor
> The Trinity in faith . . .)

The saints, full of love without desire, discuss their sufferings on
earth (stanzas 56–69), which gives Scheffler an opportunity to al-
lude to a variety of legends. Jesus himself appears (stanzas 70–
72), described in tones which remind one somewhat of the *Holy
Joy of the Soul*, but which remain muted and weak. Mary (stanza
73), the Patriarchs (stanza 74), and the Popes and Emperors
(stanza 76) also appear. After long passages of homage offered
by the saints and descriptions of their beauty (stanzas 78–89,
102–28), Christ enriches them by awarding them feudal fiefs
(stanzas 129–30)! After the banquet, God Himself appears
(stanza 143); and in the following stanza there is an unmistakable, though cautious, echo from the *Cherubinic Wanderer*:

> Sie werden da ein Gott in Gott,
> Ein Wesen, eine Wonne,
> Sie sind daselbst das Himmelsbrot
> Und selbst die ewge Sonne.
> Sie werden eine Seligkeit
> Mit ihm, ein Geist und Leben,
> Ein Licht und eine Herrlichkeit,
> Ein einiges Erheben.
>
> (Then they become a God in God,
> One being, one joy;
> They are right then the bread of Heaven,
> And themselves the eternal sun.
> They become one blessedness

> With Him, one spirit and life,
> One light and one majesty,
> One unified uplifting.)

At this point Scheffler begins his peroration by asserting that the reality of Paradise is beyond his powers of description (stanza 146). This is followed by a homily on the way to salvation, including a vague paraphrase of the Sermon on the Mount (stanzas 148–55). Scheffler, mindful as always of his hostility to the Lutherans, concludes the poem by an exhortation to good works.

Today the *Sensual Description*, were it not from the pen of Johann Scheffler, would doubtless remain unnoticed and unremembered in that vast limbo where all insignificant literature reposes. As it is, we stare at the production of a poet untrue to himself, not because he gave himself up to theology—an honorable undertaking—but because he had neither the talent nor the mind for theology, and because he sacrificed his gift for poetry. Unlike the minor or unsuccessful work of many great poets, the *Sensual Description* sheds no light on the major poems. Despite occasional echoes of other days and faint traces of other visions, it is as though Scheffler had become a different man.

CHAPTER 5

Defender of the Faith: Ecclesiologia

I *The Poet Turned Prophet*

IN 1677, the last year of his life, Scheffler collected, revised, and
published thirty-nine of his polemical and didactic pamphlets
under the title *Ecclesiologia or Description of the Church.* The
text is preceded by an engraved title page that is a curiosity even
in this age of fascinating allegory and iconography. The engraving
depicts the City of God high on a hill under attack from the heretics and defended by an angel carrying a sword with a Latin in-
scription that translates "Sword of Glory; the Test of Faith," and a
shield which reads "Shield of Assistance; the Defense of the
Faith." Hovering about the city are six other angels, bearing
swords and shields with the following inscriptions: "Tradition; In-
vincibility," "Practice of the Church; Infallibility," "The Fathers;
Identity," "Authority of the Church; Visibility," "Scripture; Universality," "Council; Perpetuity." Below the city, a devil identified
as "Heresy" leads a group of Protestants who vainly attempt to
storm the city with empty sheaths labelled "The Word of God
without the Spirit" and "The Letter without the Sense," and pens
marked "Calumny," "Mendacity," "Contumely," and "Blasphemy."
In order to spur on the heretics, Calvin stands (below left) blow-
ing a ram's horn, and a very vapid-looking Luther beats a drum
(below right). Above it all arches a motto, "The Unceasing Assistance of the Holy Spirit"; and, in order to show that the author
was inspired by the Holy Ghost, as Scheffler stresses in his rather
superfluous explanation of the allegory on the following page, a
dove descends from Heaven with the *Ecclesiologia* in its beak—no
mean feat for the dove, incidentally, for the *Ecclesiologia* is a
hefty quarto of more than 1,200 pages of heavy, good-quality
paper.

So far as the general content of the tracts is concerned, the title
page tells us all we need to know. It was remarked of the *Sensual*

Description that Scheffler did not have a well-developed theological mind. But theological subtlety was not much in demand in the seventeenth century—in a situation in which the opposing positions had been frozen for well over a hundred years. Scheffler's position is simple and rigidly orthodox: the Church is the only source of truth, faith, and salvation. The Protestants lack the authority of tradition and the support of divine signs. Furthermore, they are disunited among themselves. The Lutheran principles of justification by faith alone and the human impossibility of fulfilling God's commandments are absurd and contrary to Scripture. The individual appeal to reason in the interpretation of Scripture —and this is by far the strongest argument on the Catholic side of the debate—is treacherous and full of pitfalls. Scripture can be made to yield its true sense only under the inspiration of the Holy Ghost, and the Holy Ghost speaks only through the Church. The Protestants deny these propositions and assert the opposite. This is the main intellectual substance of the pamphlet war that had been going on intermittently since 1520; and it is no wonder that, around the turn of the eighteenth century, people began to find ways to circumvent the whole insoluble complex of issues.

That a poet, and a mystic poet at that, should spend years of his life and a great deal of his energy in publicly defending such unsophisticated propositions has been felt to be nothing short of disgraceful by succeeding generations. It should be emphasized that this opinion does not derive, at least to any significant degree, from an anti-Catholic prejudice among the critics. Had Scheffler remained in his father's faith and carried on the polemic in the same style on the Protestant side, no one would have thought the better of him. This activity seems so incongruous with the mysticism of his youth that one scholar attempted to prove, vainly to be sure, that the poet Angelus Silesius and the pamphleteer Johann Scheffler were not one and the same person.[1] Nevertheless, a look at some of the details of these works does not seem out of order, particularly as some of their most interesting features are not usually stressed in the secondary literature.[2] The man's personality must hang together somehow; and perhaps a study of the tense subservience of his later years will help to throw some light on the tentativeness of the mysticism out of which the *Cherubinic Wanderer* grew.

Scheffler asserts in his preface that in his polemical period he had written two or three tractates a year for a total of more than fifty-five (p. viii).[3] We do not know the titles of all of these, and those we do know we cannot always date because Scheffler does not give publication dates in the *Ecclesiologia,* and the originals are hard to find. Scheffler would have us believe that the polemics were written against his will and out of necessity, for he would willingly have maintained his spiritual peace and avoided the suffering he underwent from the attacks of his opponents. Only the love of Christ and the knowledge that he would be glorified in Heaven as a reward turned him to it. This disclaimer must be taken with a grain of salt. For one thing, it is part of the conventions of both sides of this polemic that the writer repeatedly asserts his distaste for the whole matter and takes up his weary pen only because he has been driven to it by the shamelessness of his opponents; for another, a man with a genuine aversion to public controversy does not publish fifty-five controversial pamphlets; and for a third, the aggressive irritability of almost all these writings belies the long-suffering pose. It is clear from their tone that Scheffler could not tolerate the idea that anyone in Christendom held religious opinions different from his own. In his case this intolerance seems less the result of the familiar fanaticism of the convert than an outgrowth of the basic insecurity of spirit that characterizes all the actions of his life. This is not to call into question his conscious motivation, which, out of the logic and presuppositions of his faith, urged him to stop at nothing to achieve the single important goal of bringing men to salvation. The Inquisition, after all, operated on the same generous principle. Scheffler cared little for his personal reputation and welfare, and in his preface he expressly offers the tractates to the public domain, in order to give them the widest possible circulation.

In his preface Scheffler makes an important distinction between didactic and polemic tracts. The former, which attempted to present the Catholic case directly to the people in a variety of ways, he now regards as a fruitful and satisfying undertaking; the latter, an endless round of hopeless quarrels among the learned, had brought him little except the feeling that he had at least not been driven from the field. Now, after fourteen years, Scheffler shows an insight into the futility of the pamphlet war. There can be no

doubt from the tone of his remarks that his spirit had been hurt
and abraded by the slashing attacks of his opponents—no matter
how often he attempts to shake them off with a sovereign gesture
—and perhaps also by a recognition that, as far as anyone can see,
he had accomplished nothing. His remarks earlier in the preface
about the lukewarm attitude of his fellow Catholics, as well as the
pathos of his own description of his decline and impending death
suggest that peace of soul had remained permanently out of his
reach.

The volume itself was printed in two parts because the printing
was going too slowly, and so the longer tractates were sent to
another firm. Both parts were then bound together. The first part
consists of twenty-nine tractates in 1,247 columns numbered with
Arabic numerals; the second part contains nine in 930 columns
designated by Roman numerals. This distinction will be maintained in the citations which follow. In addition, there are forty-
nine unnumbered pages of a highly convenient index with references to the major topics. The pages of front matter are also
unnumbered.

II *The Turkish Scourge*

In our discussion of Scheffler's career, we had occasion to mention the first of the polemics (apart from the justification of his
conversion in 1653), the bombshell of 1663 called the *Turkish
Pamphlet*. We remarked there upon the simplistic logic which ac-
tuates this work: taking as a model the interpretation of Jewish
history in the Old Testament, particularly the account of the king-
doms of Israel and Judah, Scheffler connects the advances made
by the Turks after the third decade of the sixteenth century with
the simultaneous spread of Lutheran doctrine. The idea seems absurd and horrifying to the modern mind and doubtless seemed so
also to a good many of Scheffler's contemporaries. There is a kind
of attractive boldness about it, nonetheless, which at least has the
virtue of making one inquire of himself whether he takes the Old
Testament account seriously or not; and it probably would have
remained more impressive had Scheffler allowed it simply to rest
upon its fundamentalist suppositions. But the long pamphlet,
which fills seventy columns in the *Ecclesiologia,* is an exercise in
pseudo-logic. A battery of heterogeneous arguments is marshaled

which weakens rather than strengthens the basic principle. Although Scheffler in the beginning cheerfully compares himself to a Hebrew prophet (which certainly must have revolted any Jews who came across the pamphlet), he leaves this ground immediately to argue that Germany had been civilized by the Roman Church and everything collapsed after the coming of Luther, "for it is once and for all certain, that a thing is sustained by the same thing which gave it birth" (col. iii), which seems almost a parody of scholastic argument. He goes on to maintain that rebellion is the worst of crimes in both worlds and attempts to demonstrate from New Testament sources that heresy is a form of rebellion. This charge of sedition, which was a serious one in this authoritarian age, stung the Lutherans, who occasionally threw it back in Scheffler's teeth. Scheffler then switches to a historical argument. He tries to show that a series of national disasters always followed upon heresies—an unusually naïve version of history as written by the victors—and goes extensively into the history of the Byzantine Church to argue the fall of the Eastern Empire from the same principles. Somewhat later, however, he maintains that the apparently faithful Christians in the East who have already been overcome by the infidels must have been bad Christians, for God's promise to protect the faithful cannot be vain (cols. xxxvii–xxxiix). The argument is thus completely circular, facts being adduced to support the principle where they appear to be available, and the principle being called upon for the presupposition of facts where they are not. Scheffler returns to the Byzantine example in another connection when he asserts that the Greeks went down because of the polyglot, cosmopolitan character of their forces. Whatever validity that observation may have, there can be no doubt that he has a point when he argues that the internal disunities caused by the Reformation prevented the Empire from meeting the Turkish threat with sufficient energy. Scheffler accuses Luther of having advised the Protestant princes to weaken the Emperor by not supporting him against the Truks.

One of the strangest examples of Scheffler's argumentation appears in what is clearly an addendum to the *Turkish Pamphlet* written for the *Ecclesiologia*. It is a reply to Johann Adam Schertzer's sharp-witted if slightly disingenuous rejoinder that Scheffler had applied the same method of argument against the Protestants as the Roman traditionalists had used against the Christians, namely that this heresy was bringing troubles upon the Empire. To this Scheffler replies:

The pagans ascribed the plagues to the Christians because they thought that they had fallen away from the worship of the immortal gods for the worship of a hanged man; but they could not demonstrate with a single example that the peoples who had previously fallen away from these putative gods and worshipped a hanged man as God had been punished with such plagues: for this had not happened since the beginning of the world. Therefore this accusation consisted of mere delusion (col. xliix.).

Scheffler's customary lucidity seems to have failed him slightly at this point; but it is the weirdness of the argument itself that is most likely to be baffling. The key to it is Scheffler's belief in the efficacy of argument from past authority. This was an intellectual position widely, indeed, almost universally held in the seventeenth century, as it had been in past ages; and the controversies of the Reformation turned not upon authority versus independent thinking, but upon the relative merits of competing authority. But Scheffler's adherence to the principles, as to all his intellectual positions, is outrageously extreme. Reduced to the simplest terms, the argument is as follows: (a) Schertzer has compared unlikes, because (b) Scheffler has been arguing from recorded past events, whereas (c) the Romans could not demonstrate that something exactly similar had ever happened before; that is, it had never occurred that people had deserted the pagan gods for a hanged man and suffered divine penalty for it. Therefore (d) the Roman accusation lacks substance. If this seems like stacking the deck rather shamelessly, Scheffler then goes himself one better by blandly pointing out that, after all, the hanged man *was* God, thus reducing the whole exchange to nonsense.

At one point in the pamphlet war, about a year after publication of the *Turkish Pamphlet,* Schertzer quite testily pointed out that after all he was a learned theologian and Scheffler was not; Scheffler howled at this, and Schertzer replied: "What would it bother me if Scheffler were to say I didn't know anything about medicine?" [4] Schertzer is right in a way, for, as we have seen by now, Scheffler's "theology" is an argumentative hodgepodge. But

Schertzer nevertheless fails to convince us and not only because the arguments on the Protestant side seldom look much better to modern eyes or because the whole debate has ceased to interest us. For the poet Scheffler unquestionably has the advantage of expression over his opponents. His language is much clearer and more elegant (Schertzer's syntax is often difficult to unravel), his images are bolder, his ideas wilder, and his textures richer. His polemic style is not restricted to empty invective but disposes of a wide range of exotic weapons, of which the above passage on the Romans is a particularly outlandish but not isolated example. Thus Scheffler's strengths and weaknesses as a polemicist are related in a curious way. It is axiomatic that a mystic does not belong in the realm of rigorous logical discourse; and by attempting to operate in this realm, Scheffler became a creature neither fish nor fowl.

Toward the end of the *Turkish Pamphlet* Scheffler resorts to a set of arguments quite various in their quality. He castigates the Christian Empire for not preserving unity and stresses the unity and purposiveness of Islam and its belief in spreading the faith by violence in terms quite reminiscent of the official attitude of the Western world toward the Communist menace in the 1950's. Like that argument, Scheffler's seems overwrought and politically insensitive, especially in the context in which it appears, but, also like the latter-day version, it obviously contained enough truth to make it at least discussable. Scheffler's next point, however, is offensive by its sheer ingratitude. It had been objected that in Holland the faiths were tolerated side by side and that nevertheless the Dutch continued to live in peace and prosperity. Scheffler, conveniently ignoring his own days in Holland and the impetus which he had undoubtedly received from the rich and varied religious life there, replied that it was too soon to tell, that God's revenge for this tolerance would surely strike Holland eventually. The fear of new ideas of religious toleration is a theme that was to acquire increasing importance in Scheffler's pamphlets. From this point Scheffler goes on to argue that the Protestants are in fact themselves on the way toward becoming Turks. This argument, which includes an added performance of logic-chopping in reply to Schertzer, is too foolish to reproduce. It is constructed on the pattern: the Turks deny the authority of the Pope, so do the Prot-

estants, *ergo* the Protestants are becoming Turks. The final peroration, blithely indifferent to the previous picture of the unified
might of Islam, stresses the weakness of the Turks in order to
encourage the spirit of the Germans.

III   *The People of God*

We have spent some time with the *Turkish Pamphlet,* partly
because its style and procedure are fairly typical of Scheffler's
writings in this genre, and partly because it is one of his two most
important polemic pamphlets, the other being the frontal attack
upon tolerance to which we shall come presently. Space restricts
us to a few remarks upon the notable features of the other works.
One of these is the *Christen-Schrifft / von dem herrlichen Kenn-
zeichen deß Volkes GOttes / und der wunderbahren Errettung der
Christen (Christian Pamphlet on the Magnificent Characteristics
of the People of God and the Miraculous Rescue of the Christians,*
col. lxix–cxxxiix), a more positive version of the *Turkish Pamphlet*
that recapitulates its arguments and attempts to show, largely
with legendary stories of miracles, that the faithful have always
been rescued by divine intervention. Scheffler's lack of critical
acumen in the use of these materials is most evident here. He
carries the stories of wonderful fortune into quite modern times;
and, because of the reported appearance of Mary in a dream,
even the slippery politics attending the election of Emperor Ferdinand II in 1619 are accounted among them. The Protestants, he
argues, are losing ground to the Counter Reformation because
they cannot show such miracles. Scheffler's lack of sensitivity to
human psychology is evident in a story he tells of Henry of
Navarre (1553–1610), later the brilliant King Henry IV of
France. Henry, it is said, asked the Calvinists whether he could
also be saved in the Catholic faith, to which they agreed. The
Catholics, on the other hand, denied that he could be saved in the
Calvinist religion. Thus Henry reasoned, in Scheffler's words,
" 'You say that I can be saved in the Catholic faith and the Catholics say so also; on the other hand, you are the only ones who say
that I can be saved in the Calvinist faith, whereas they do not;
thus I will do better if I follow the testimony of both of you rather
than one alone.' Thereupon he became Catholic" (col. cxiii).
Scheffler completely misses the cynical wit of this argument and

turns it in all seriousness against the Protestants. Furthermore, he does not seem to care whether his witness was an appropriate person for his purposes or not. Surely most of the educated and alert people of Europe must have understood that it was considerations of power politics that caused Henry to change his religion three times; and, more seriously than that, there had hardly been a ruler in Europe who had moved further in the direction of that religious toleration Scheffler so feared and hated than Henry IV. This is significant because the tenth chapter of the *Christian Pamphlet* brings an argument in high rhetoric against political friendship between religions, "for its result is to make a *Mischmasch* out of the true and false faith and can thereby quite obscure the true one" (col. cxxi). Tolerance is a sign of lukewarm faith, he remarks with some justice; and he who can stand with God's enemy can also stand with the Devil.

There is another passage of major interest in the *Christian Pamphlet*. It is an epilogue in reply to his opponents Schertzer and Christian Chemnitz, who in their Protestant sobriety had questioned the plausibility of his miraculous legends. This raises the dangerous issue of the validity of past authority; and Scheffler, with that blind courage so characteristic of him, rose to the challenge. He begins with an argument *ad hominem,* which decorously skirts slanderous insult: "How will Chemnitius prove to me that he is the son of his father Chemnitius? In no other way, than that he has always been considered so and no honorable man has contradicted it" (col. cxxxiii); the proof, says Scheffler, that something always considered true is not true lies with him who disbelieves it. But now Scheffler advances onto ground on which most of his contemporaries would have feared to tread. He points out that if one were to go on debunking in this way, the next step would be the denial of Scripture itself (col. cxxxv). There is no rational defense, writes Scheffler, to the charge that the Bible is all fable. How plausible are the assertions that Moses wrote an account of his own death at the end of Deuteronomy, or that Joshua made the sun stand still? All this is brave enough for the man of faith, but the train of thought must have frightened him all the same, because in the remainder of the epilogue he talks himself into a rage that has no parallel in his writings. He falsely accuses the Italian reformer Bernardino Ochino (1487–1565) of setting Moses, Christ, and Mohammed equal and calling them all swindlers, and he draws a strange parallel between the Lutherans and the Samaritans, about which latter he obviously knew nothing whatever. He concludes with a series of short, sharp questions that are supposed to parody the process of debunking Scripture. He resorts, naturally, to the authority of the divine light: "If it were not for this, one could doubt all the Prophets and would, as I have said, have destroyed the entire Holy Writ" (col. cxxxiix). So Scheffler's stubbornly medieval and fundamentalist mind unwittingly produced a prophecy of the intellectual history of the next two centuries. Schertzer's dogmatic answer, incidentally, that the Holy Ghost guarantees Scripture but not the legends,[5] hardly seems equal to the profundity of the issue Scheffler has raised.

IV *The Idolatry of Reason*

In the most lucid part of his intellect, Scheffler was able to see that the fundamental difference between Catholics and Protestants lay not so much in specific issues of dogma, but in the question of authority. The Reformation, he saw, had subjected the propositions of religion to the workings of the rational mind, not to the extent that we are used to four hundred and fifty years later, but sufficiently to deny the validity of the cumulative tradition within the Church. Consequently he attempted to kill two birds with one stone: he picked up the Protestant charge of idolatry, which had been leveled against the Catholic Church with Old Testament earnestness, and turned it against the Protestants by asserting that they worshiped an idol of reason. Scheffler's pamphlet *Der Lutheraner und Calvinisten Abgott d[er] Vernunft* (*The Lutherans' and Calvinists' Idol of Reason, ca.* 1667, cols. ccclxv–cdlxxvi) argues that the Protestants are idolators because their God is a creation of man's reason, which is then adored. His main point is the arbitrariness of Protestant exegesis; and a large part of the pamphlet is devoted to familiar arguments on justification by faith alone and the Catholic homage to the saints. At one point, however, Scheffler argues rather interestingly that this kind of idolatry must lead to diabolism because of the inconstancy of individual reason:

For because it is impossible that man should stand on nothing; the idol, however, as an image of the reason is a nothing, so he does not remain constant to this image, but rather makes it first one way, then another, until finally, through this distortion, he completely departs from the image of the true God of whom he had originally still retained many features (cols. cdxxxiix–cdxxxix).

V *The Attack on Political Solutions*

Scheffler's adherence to the principle of the Counter Reformation was absolute. Since the Protestants are condemned to eternal damnation, Christian charity requires that every effort be made to bring them back to the True Church; and it is part of the sacred responsibility of princes toward their subjects to pursue this end. This effort, however, is hindered by political considerations, first of all by the legal arrangements which had been made within the Empire to neutralize the strife somewhat, and secondly by what was evidently a growing willingness to separate the religious and political realms. Scheffler, now more than ever assuming the role of an Old Testament prophet, attempted to combat both these forces. In the principalities of Silesia, as in other places of the Empire, an important keystone in the structure of Protestantism was the Augsburg Confession. This document was composed at the Diet of Augsburg in 1530 by Philipp Melanchthon in one of the most beleaguered and unsteady hours in his sometimes not very courageous career. At that time it was rejected by the emperor; but after the Protestant princes had fought the emperor to a standstill, it was written into the Peace of Augsburg in 1555, which gave principalities that adhered to the Confession (and no other sects) important rights of existence within the Empire. When compared with the aggressive *élan* of the Reformation generally, the Augsburg Confession must be seen as a most cautious compromise. It did not then, nor did it in the seventeenth century, strongly affirm the Protestant theological position. It had been written, in fact, to minimize rather than stress differences in doctrine. It did not mention universal priesthood, nor did it challenge papal supremacy, indulgences, purgatory, or the sacraments.[6] Scheffler pounced on the weaknesses of this document, and in three bitter pamphlets[7] argued that the Lutherans had forfeited their rights in Silesia because their doctrines did not coincide with those of the Augsburg Confession. He stressed particularly the issue of the Pope's authority. Consequently, he argued, the road was open to a legal suppressiion of Protestantism in Silesia.

That Scheffler detected an increasing secularization of political thinking is evident from his pamphlet *Spiegel der Ketzerey* (*Mirror of Heresy,* cols. 1182–1221). In the title he advertises "a short confutation of 'politicism' as the most pernicious heresy," which he gives in the thirty-seventh chapter of this otherwise uninspired tract. The attitude of the *politici,* that is, of those who place political considerations above the absolute demands of faith, implies, he argues, that all the sects together are Christendom and that one may have any opinion he likes. This means in turn that the majority of Christian mankind in all past ages were fools. In this way Scheffler rejects out of hand the possibility of the development of a legitimate new idea. He makes it clear, however, that he sees chiefly the negative side of this development, that is, that a substantial lack of interest in religious considerations generally is the source of tolerance.

For these heretics [the *politici*] say that fighting about religion is only unnecessary priestly wrangling and foolishness. If one is only basically in agreement and believes in Christianity, then one need take no interest in one another. All can equally achieve salvation. Therefore, according to the occasion, they externally hold sometimes with one religion and sometimes with another. In their hearts, however, they laugh at them all (col. 1215).

Here we are at the diametrically opposite pole from the ecumenical movement of the mid-twentieth century.

VI *The Perniciousness of Tolerance*

All of these ideas were most thoroughly adumbrated in Scheffler's major contribution to the cause of human bondage, *Gerechtfertigter Gewissenszwang oder Erweiß daß man die Ketzer zum wahren Glauben zwingen könne und solle* (*Coercion of Conscience Justified, or Proof that One Can and Should Force the Heretics to the True Faith,* 1673, cols. dclxv–dcclvi). The pamphlet is addressed to Emperor Leopold I, who in the wake of the rebellion of the magnates had roughly suppressed the Protestants in Hungary, although Scheffler must have known as well as anyone else that what could be done in Hungary could not necessarily be done against the well-entrenched Protestant princes in Germany. Quite early in the pamphlet Scheffler shows his awareness that he disagrees with many of his contemporaries: "I have taken up a cause (to be sure not from my own motives but from the impulse of a Christian zealot), which brings me the greatest hostility among the heretics, and among many Catholics nothing but calumny and disfavor" (col. dclxvii). With a certain show of objectivity, Scheffler begins by listing the arguments against coercion of conscience, chiefly that God wants a free-will offering, that the Scriptural parable of the wheat and the tares argues against it, and that coercion produces only hypocrites. But more serious considerations outweigh these: heresy is the worst of all vices because it damages immortal souls and injures and robs the Church; all heretical teaching is blasphemy because the Church's doctrine is a revelation of the Holy Ghost; and followers of heresy should be punished with "a horrible death" (col. dclxxx). The Church is master of the conscience and is bound in love to maintain that position: "Should the Church be such an unmerciful mother that she allows all her children to be swallowed by the Devil and does not take up the worldly sword to prevent this evil?" (col. dclxxxi). Peter, after all, was only asked to put up his sword, not to throw it away. Drawing richly from past authority, Scheffler gives a series of examples of persecutions carried on by the Church to show that such persecution was traditional and therefore justified. It is no wonder that he made some of his allies nervous. We are reminded of Bert Brecht, in his play *The Measures Taken* (1930), scaring the daylights out of the Communist Party by loyally making the logic of its doctrine of revolution visible to all on the stage.

Scheffler is willing to acknowledge the force of the argument that to put conscience under duress leads naturally to hypocrisy; but he urges that nevertheless the chances of saving souls are better this way, for that which is begun out of fear may end in love, and the forced Catholic may become willing. With questionable psychological insight he adds: "A father has after all as much pleasure in a son whom he has forced to obedience with the fear of punishment as in one who has always been freely obedient" (col. dclxxxv). The issue of obedience is an important one for Scheffler, for he regularly sees heresy in terms of atrocious rebellion against authority. This has the curious result that he actually denies the Church the right to force conversion upon pagans and Jews. He was, of course, by no means friendly to the Jews—in one of his more foolish moments he suggested to the Hebrew scholar Schertzer that professors of Hebrew should be circumcised [8]—but on the whole his attitude toward them is about as mild as it well could be. Later in the *Coercion of Conscience* (Chapter XXI), he asserts that the Jews are tolerated in the hope of conversion, as witnesses to the Passion and to the prophecy of it. Like most partisan zealots, Scheffler reserves his fury for those who deviate the least from the position he holds.

In a number of chapters making up about the middle third of the pamphlet, Scheffler brings forth a series of political arguments suffused with theological and homiletic considerations. Some of these observations are not without a certain cynicism. In Chapters VII and VIII he points out that the early Church did not carry on persecutions only because it lacked the power to do so; and in Chapter XIII he advises, rationally but not very attractively, that one should not try to suppress the heretics when they are strong, but only when one is superior. So far as the trauma of the Thirty Years' War is concerned, Scheffler dismisses the grief about it as sentimentality. In Chapter XIV he asserts that the devastation of the land caused by persecution is unimportant *sub specie aeternitatis;* and in any case God has promised to preserve the land of the faithful. Better a devastated land than the continued existence of heretics. Moreover, heretics are dangerous because their rebellious temperament also threatens the authority of the state. Chapter XV picks up the argument from the *Turkish Pamphlet* that heresy in fact leads to the destruction of the state and reaches back into history to show how new doctrines weakened ancient Rome and, more recently, the Turkish Empire. The rebellion of the Netherlands, which even for such conservatives as Goethe and Schiller was a heroic undertaking, is seen by Scheffler from the point of view of Spain's loss—what the Netherlanders were actually fighting for appears to be entirely beyond his ken.

From this point of view, Scheffler sees his own age, which to us seems so violent and inhumane, as one of feeble decadence. After recounting some of the brutal procedures of the early emperors against the heretics, he comments: "My God, if at the present time an emperor were to give such orders, what would there not be for an outcry about the devastation of the land! How much sympathy would not many people feel that the poor people were being so persecuted!" (col. dccxxiv). His outrage makes us feel warmer toward his contemporaries than we otherwise might. Scheffler almost makes us believe in the moral progress of the human race—inadvertently, to be sure.

Some of this extremism apparently arises out of the frustrations of the evangelist, the feeling that the whole technique of argument and polemic is fruitless; and Scheffler makes an observation that reflects sadly on his own publicistic career: "If one wants to preach to them, they don't come to church, or if they do, with uncircumcised ears and hearts. If one writes books, they don't buy them. If one tries to give the books to them, they do not want to accept them or read them" (col. dccxxxi). This is the closest Scheffler comes anywhere to understanding the pride of the individual and his reluctance to be bullied by the self-righteous.

It is possible that in the course of writing the pamphlet Scheffler began to become aware of his own horrifying tone. In Chapter XX he begins to moderate his tirade against peaceful coexistence; and although he continually takes back with one hand what he gives with the other, he indicates some hesitations in his remark, so absurd coming from his pen, that one should not make enemies of the heretics, for one must after all live with them, but that one should have nothing to do with them in any context, including the political. Later he points out with some justification that the heretics themselves believe in coercion of conscience (he is no doubt thinking particularly of Calvin) and states that it is obviously permissible to execute heretics. Here he seems to have frightened himself somewhat, for he remarks almost immediately that he does not want to incite to killing. On the other hand, it is better if a few die for the sake of the spiritual health of the people as a whole. In order to demonstrate that he is not excessively bloodthirsty, he supplies some hair-raising quotations from Luther on the subject and caps his argument with the familiar justification of the Inquisition that death in this world pales into insignificance when compared to the awfulness of eternal damnation.

Having addressed the beginning of the pamphlet to Emperor Leopold, Scheffler turns to the princes of the Empire in an epilogue (Chapter XXIV) that exhibits what is in a way his most admirable characteristic: his complete lack of subservience to human authority. There is not a major figure in German literature of this period who, when the occasion arises, speaks of the noble, the highborn, and the powerful with less cringing and sycophancy than Scheffler. The only thing remotely like it is Gryphius' critique of arbitrary political power in his drama *Papinianus* (1659). Scheffler's argument is, to be sure, not revolutionary. It rests upon the responsibility of the prince to strive for the welfare of his subjects. If the princes, so he argues, refrain from forcing the faith on their subjects, they lack zeal and Christian love because they allow them to fall into damnation. It is the tone in which he addresses the potentates which is out of the ordinary: "Indeed, you give one to understand that only the belly is your God, and the purse your idol" (col. dcclv).

VII *The Popular Touch*

In turning from the polemic tracts to the didactic pamphlets, one hopes that the harshness of the former might be relieved with a little warmth, especially in view of Scheffler's own claim that his more popular writings gave him greater satisfaction. On the whole this hope is disappointed. The didactic pamphlets have some interesting features, but their general tone is colored by the typical disdain of the learned for the ordinary mortal. A number of these pamphlets are in the form of dialogues in which the weaker Protestant positions are overrun by familiar Catholic arguments. An example is the short pamphlet entitled *Simplicii Angeregte Ursachen Warumb er nicht Catholisch werden könne. Von Bonamico In einem Gespräche widerlegt* (*Simplicius' Interesting Reasons Why He Could Not Become Catholic, Refuted in a Conversation with Bonamicus,* cols. 824–41). Simplicius is, as his name indicates, a simple man, who holds to Lutheran doctrines he does not understand, whereas Bonamicus, contrary to his name, does not deal with him in a very friendly manner. They carry on a rather lively debate, but it seems in fact a wish-dream on the part of Scheffler, because Simplicius yields with such ease. An example of the flavor of this dialogue is found in the following passage:

Bonamic.: . . . Now what do you have against the mass?
Simplic.: I say that it is a right abominable idolatry.
Bonamic.: Why is it idolatry?
Simplic.: Because you carry on such abominable idolatry in it.
Bonamic.: What sort of abominable idolatry do we carry on in it?
Simplic.: Oh, what do I care! I have heard that you carry on atrocious idolatry with it; you crucify Christ in it anew.
Bonamic.: It seems that you are a right crude calf, not to say ox, that you slander what you do not understand and abuse the mass which you don't even know. What is the mass?
Simplic.: What is that to me? (col. 836).

Thus defeated, Simplicius receives a lecture on the Mass from Bonamicus, and, unable to hold his own ground, is eventually converted.

The odd thing about this learned superciliousness of the Catholic apologete is that in another pamphlet Scheffler accuses the Lutheran side of precisely that failing. In *Der Catholisch gewordene Bauer* (*The Peasant Become Catholic*, cols. 886–901), it is the peasant, firm in his Catholic faith, who refutes the blandishments of a Lutheran clergyman. In his frustration this worthy is made to say: "You are an unlearned peasant, you do not understand what truth is. But I am a learned man, I understand it" (col. 893). There can be little doubt that Scheffler had his enemy Schertzer in mind when he wrote this passage, because Schertzer was inclined to take this attitude toward the amateur Catholic theologian.

Another variation on this theme, however, seems all but inexplicable in view of the purpose of these writings. In a tract entitled *Die kluge Frau* (*The Clever Woman*, cols. 920–29), a Catholic priest carries on a dialogue with a peasant woman whose husband has become Catholic. She, however, remains obdurate in her Lutheran faith; and the curious thing about the pamphlet is that the priest utterly fails to move her:

Woman: . . . Although to be sure no one has made me a doctor, still I have read Scripture from my childhood on and have learned many fine sayings out of it. I know very well what I should believe, and also have, thank God, enough sense to be able to distinguish between black and white. I can see very well what is Scripture or not Scripture.

[154]

Priest: May the woman excuse me, but it is just these people who imagine that they can understand the Holy Scripture by themselves without a master whom St. Augustine calls fools.
Woman: That doesn't concern me; Augustine may say what he likes, I will remain with the clear word of God (col. 922).

The priest tries to cut her down as a mere woman, but he fails. He only angers her when he insists she cannot have a man's understanding. This taxes the priest's patience and puts an end to his politeness: "Oh dear lady, do not crow so loud. It is an evil omen when the hens begin to crow" (col. 926). But it is all to no avail, and finally the woman drives the priest from her sight. Just what Scheffler thought to accomplish by publishing this amusing but rather unedifying dialogue is hard to make out. Is it possible that there is here a strange breakthrough of Scheffler's literary temperament, that the urge to tell a realistic story despite its doctrinal inappropriateness ran away with him? Perhaps. It seems more likely, however, that Scheffler depended upon the universal intellectual contempt for women and was certain that the clever woman would be regarded as a horrible example without further explanation.

VIII *The Vanished Mystic*

Taken all in all, the *Ecclesiologia* is a sad business. Its theology is not worthy of the mind that produced the *Cherubinic Wanderer,* and the obvious opposition of Scheffler's pamphlets to what were some of the more hopeful ideas arising out of a tormented age is painful. Despite its undeniably interesting features—it is amazing, given the subject and the tone of these writings, how often they manage to hold the attention of even an unsympathetic reader—it must be booked with such egregious wastes of genius as the years Isaac Newton spent trying to unravel the prophecies of Daniel. Scheffler's case is the more pathetic because his fanatic zeal so obviously grew out of weaknesses in his spiritual and intellectual manhood. Rather than dare to unleash his mystical imagination completely, he shrank before the uncertainty of his own labile mind and chose the path of intellectual abdication. I do not wish to make it appear that this is the necessary result of allegiance to the Catholic Church. Many famous converts have car-

ried their imaginative intellects with them into the Church un-
compromised. Scheffler did not.

Posterity has often been astonished at Scheffler's polemic career. What, people have asked, became of the mystical vision that
inspired him in his youth? The question, put this way, is not difficult to solve, for Scheffler himself answers it in *The Lutherans'
and Calvinists' Idol of Reason:*

Now it is all the same whether I imagine God as an old man or a king
or as a delightful light or as an immeasurable essence like pure air or
as a sea of all joy in which is all sweetness or as a lovely dawn or as
high as ever I can; still it is an image. For God is not all these things.
Indeed he is not all those things which I can imagine in my mortality
(col. cdxlv).

Here Scheffler has taken one of the major insights of mysticism
and reduced it to indifference. He has lost all interest in spiritual
aspiration; and the various possibilities, which to the mystic mean
attempts to reach beyond the natural limits of the mind, are here
soberly reviewed. The mystic presumes faith, but here, in the face
of the doctrinal issue of faith, the higher possibilities have become
unimportant. That is what became of Scheffler's mystical substance. How it happened, no one will ever exactly know.

Notes and References

Chapter One

1. Angelus Silesius. *Sämtliche poetische Werke in drei Bänden,* ed. Hans Ludwig Held (3rd ed.; Munich: Hanser, 1952), I, 14. Hereinafter cited as Held.
2. Held, I, 16–17.
3. Lessing published an edition of Scultetus' poems in 1771. See Held, I, 119, n. 21.
4. Held, I, 215–16.
5. Held, II, 7.
6. Held, II, 7–9.
7. Held, II, 22–23.
8. Held, II, 10–12.
9. Held, II, 13–22.
10. Held, I, 118, n. 19.
11. Held, I, 27.
12. Held, I, 121, n. 26.
13. Johann Adam Schertzer, *Und Scheffler redet noch so viel als nichts/ oder Johannis Schefflers übelschmähende und seine Christen-Schrifft so viel als nichts schützende Schutz-Rede* (Leipzig: Friederich Lanckisch, 1664), p. 4; Held, I, 121, n. 26.
14. Held, I, 307–14.
15. Schertzer, *Und Scheffler redet noch so viel als nichts,* p. [viii].
16. The chief defender of this view is Carl Seltmann, Dean of the Cathedral of Breslau, in his study *Angelus Silesius und seine Mystik* (Breslau: G. P. Aderholz, 1896). He is supported by the Jesuit Karl Richstätter in three articles, "Angelus Silesius, Mystiker und Konvertit," *Stimmen der Zeit,* CXI (1926), 361–81; "Angelus Silesius und sein jüngstes Lebensbild," *Zeitschrift für Askese und Mystik,* III (1927), 79–85; and "Barocke Mystik des Angelus Silesius," *Stimmen der Zeit,* CXXI (1931), 326–40. The arguments of Scheffler's Catholic apologetes and their various refutations are too involved to be treated here;

see Held, I, 33–37, and Rudolf Neuwinger, *Johann Schefflers "Cherubinischer Wandersmann" und die deutsche Mystik* (Blecherode am Harz: Nieft, 1937), pp. 26–31.

17. Held, I, 121, n. 26.

18. Held, I, 25.

19. Diploma in Held, I, 223–27.

20. Georg Ellinger, *Angelus Silesius. Ein Lebensbild* (Breslau: Wilh. Gottl. Korn, 1927), pp. 41–42. Hereinafter cited as Ellinger, *Lebensbild.*

21. Held, I, 23.

22. See Ellinger, *Lebensbild,* p. 29.

23. For this and other facts of his life, see Held I, 122–23, n. 22.

24. Quoted Held, I, 123.

25. Held, I, 27.

26. Held, I, 18.

27. Held, I, 30.

28. Ellinger, *Lebensbild,* pp. 44–46.

29. Held, II, 23–27.

30. Held, I, 231.

31. Held, I, 30.

32. Just why Scheffler took this name and used it in this form is not entirely clear. As a matter of course he took a new Christian name on the occasion of his conversion to Catholicism; and it has been suggested that he chose "Angelus" after a sixteenth-century Spanish mystic, Johannes ab Angelis, and used the epithet "Silesius" to distinguish himself from the Lutheran theologian Johann Angelus in Darmstadt. Even the priest who gave the eulogy at his funeral, however, dwells on the symbolic significance of the name. See Held, I, 38; 127, nn. 48, 49; 342.

33. Text in Held, I, 233–54.

34. Chemnitz' Latin title translates as follows: *Truth of the Lutheran Religion Defended, or Examination of the Arguments and Bases with which Dr. Johann Scheffler Combats Our Religion and by Which He has Testified in a Public Pamphlet He Was Moved to Apostasy.* See Ellinger, *Lebensbild,* p. 134.

35. Patent in Held, I, 255–57.

36. Angelus Silesius, *Selections from the Cherubinic Wanderer,* trans. J. E. Crawford Flitch (London: George Allen & Unwin Ltd., 1932), p. 24. Hereinafter cited as Flitch.

37. Avancinus gave his approbation on April 2, 1657. See Held, I, 130, n. 53.

38. In the preface (Held, I, 314).

39. Ellinger, *Lebensbild,* pp. 113–14. There have been a number of other hypotheses concerning the dates. Among the best argued are Grethe Wagner Petersen, "Zur Datierung und Deutung von Angelus Silesius: 'Cherubinischer Wandersmann,'" *Orbis litterarum,* III (1945), 139–87, and Horst Althaus, *Johann Schefflers "Cherubinischer Wandersmann": Mystik und Dichtung,* Beiträge zur deutschen Philologie, Vol. IX (Giessen: Wilhelm Schmitz, 1956), p. 2.

40. Ellinger, *Lebensbild,* p. 154.

41. Held, I, 43–44.

42. Held, I, 47.

43. Held, I, 47–48.

44. Held, I, 49–50.

45. All references to Scheffler's pamphlets are to the copy of his collection of 1677, *Der H. Römischen Kirchen Pristers Ecclesiologia Oder Kirch-Be-schreibung* (Neiss and Glatz: Ignatius Const. Schubart, 1677), in the Beinecke Rare Book Library of Yale University. The full title of this pamphlet is *Der Lutheraner und Calvinisten Abgott d[er] Vernunft* (cols. ccclxv–cdlxxvi).

46. *Des Römischen Bapsts Oberhaubtmanschaft* (*Ecclesiologia,* cols. ccxxix–ccclxvi).

47. *Gründliche Außführung/ Daß die Lutheraner auf keine Weise noch wege ihren Glauben in der Schrifft zu zeigen vermögen* (*Ecclesiologia,* cols. cdlxxvii–dclxvi).

48. Ellinger, *Lebensbild,* pp. 186–187.

49. *Kurtze Erörterung der Frage/ Ob die Lutheraner in Schlesien/ der in Instrumento Pacis denen Augsburgischen Confessions-Verwandten verliehenen Religions-Freyheit/ sich getrösten können* (*Ecclesiologia,* cols. dcclvii–dcclxxvi). Two other pamphlets on the same subject followed immediately.

50. *Ecclesiologia,* p. [viii].

51. Ellinger, *Lebensbild,* p. 210.

52. Scheffler's eulogist, the Jesuit Daniel Schwartz, refers to it as *Libellus desideriorum Joannis Amati* (Held, I, 346).

53. *Ecclesiologia,* p. [vii].

54. *Engel-Art an dem Leben und Wandel Deß WolEhrwürdigen, in Gott andächtigen, WolEdel gebohrnen, Hochgelehrten Herren Joannis Angeli Scheffler, Philosophiae und Medicinae Doctoris* (Breslau: Gottfried Gründer, 1677); reprinted Held, I, 341–54.

Chapter Two

1. Held, I, 314.

2. Ellinger, *Lebensbild,* pp. 113–14.

3. *Japanese Haiku* (Mount Vernon, New York: Peter Pauper Press, 1956), p. [57]. Quoted by permission of the Peter Pauper Press.

4. David Baumgardt, *Great Western Mystics. Their Lasting Significance* (New York: Columbia University Press, 1961), p. 7.

5. William James, *The Varieties of Religious Experience* (New York: The Modern Library, n.d.), pp. 371–72.

6. Jakob Böhme, *Sämmtliche Werke*, ed. K. W. Schiebler (Leipzig: Johann Ambrosius Barth, 1831–47), IV, 453.

7. All quotations are from the original second edition of the *Cherubinischer Wandersmann oder Geist-Reiche Sinn- und Schluß-Reime* (Glatz: Ignatius Schubarth, 1675) in the Beinecke Rare Book Library of Yale University.

8. See Rudolf Neuwinger, *Johann Schefflers "Cherubinischer Wandersmann" und die deutsche Mystik* (Blecherode am Harz: Carl Nieft, 1937), p. 174.

9. See *The Life of the Blessed Henry Suso, by Himself,* trans. T. F. Knox (London: Methuen & Co. Ltd., 1913).

10. Held, I, 121.

11. Held, I, 307.

12. See M. Hildburgis Gies, *Eine lateinische Quelle zum "Cherubinischen Wandersmann" des Angelus Silesius. Untersuchung der Beziehungen zwischen der mystischen Dichtung Scheffler und der "Clavis pro theologia mystica" des Maximilian Sandaeus,* Breslauer Studien zur historischen Theologie, Vol. XII (Breslau: Müller & Seiffert, 1929).

13. Franz Kern, *Johann Scheffler's Cherubinischer Wandersmann. Eine literarhistorische Untersuchung* (Leipzig: S. Hirzel, 1866), p. 94.

14. Joachim H. Seyppel, "Freedom and the Mystical Union in *Der cherubinische Wandersmann,*" *Germanic Review,* XXXII (1957), p. 105. To this it should be added that, in Scheffler's view, it is man who turns away and not God, whose immanence is not capricious.

15. See Held, I, p. 157, n. 99.

16. For a discussion of this aspect of Czepko's religious thought see Daniel von Czepko, *Geistliche Schriften,* ed. Werner Milch (2nd ed.; Darmstadt: Wissenschaftliche Buchgesellschaft, 1963), pp. xxxi–xxxiv. All the quotations from Czepko are taken from this edition.

17. *Ibid.,* p. 201.

18. Permission to quote Flitch's translation was obtained from the publisher, George Allen & Unwin Ltd.

19. Bilger's translations are from *Alexandrines Translated from the "Cherubinischer Wandersmann" of Angelus Silesius 1657,* (North Montpelier, Vt.: The Driftwind Press, 1944). I am indebted to the kindness of Mrs. Walter J. Coates of North Montpelier, Vt., for permission to quote these translations.

20. Martin Opitz, *Buch von der Deutschen Poeterey*, ed. Wilhelm Braune (4th ed.; Tübingen: Max Niemeyer, 1954), pp. 37–38.

21. For more detailed studies of Scheffler's form, see Benno von Wiese, "Die Antithetik in den Alexandrinern des Angelus Silesius," *Euphorion*, XXIX (1928), 503–22; and Elisabeth Spörri, *Der Cherubinische Wandersmann als Kunstwerk* (Horgen: Fritz Frei, 1947).

22. "Negative theology"—the denial that qualities can be predicated to God and to the divine substance—was introduced into the Christian tradition by the so-called Dionysius the Areopagite, an extremely gifted mystical writer who was originally identified as the Dionysius whom Paul converted at Athens (Acts 17:34), but is now known to be a Palestinian Neoplatonist of the fifth or sixth century. For a discussion of the importance of Dionysius for the tradition see Neuwinger, pp. 119–20, and Baumgardt, *Great Western Mystics*, pp. 41–46.

23. Spörri, p. 37.

24. *Eine Deutsche Theologie,* trans. Joseph Bernhart (Leipzig: Insel-Verlag, 1922), p. 205, n. 72. The author of this interesting document is unknown, calling himself only "Der Frankfurter." The earliest extant manuscript bears the date 1497, but it must be much earlier, since it was known to Tauler, who died in 1361. It is remarkable for its clarity and gentleness, and for the absolute refusal of the author to place himself in the center of attraction, qualities not all mystics possess.

25. *Ibid.,* p. 144.

26. The observer who is bound up in the thought patterns of Western language is in difficulties at this point. Neither the word "characteristic," nor the word "is" is quite correct here. For a discussion of this problem see Alfred Korzybski, *Science and Sanity* (Lancaster, Pa., and New York: The International Non-Aristotelian Library Publishing Company [1933]), *passim*, esp. Ch. IV.

27. Carus' translations are from Angelus Silesius, *A Selection from the Rhymes of a German Mystic,* trans. Paul Carus (Chicago: The Open Court Publishing Company, 1909).

28. Trask's translations are from Angelus Silesius, *The Cherubinic Wanderer. Selections,* trans. Willard R. Trask, with an introduction by Curt von Faber du Faur (New York: Pantheon Books, Inc., 1953). Quoted by permission of Random House, Inc.

29. See Althaus, *Johann Schefflers "Cherubinischer Wandersmann,"* pp. 34–35.

30. Meister Eckhart, *Deutsche Predigten und Traktate,* ed. Josef Quint (Munich: Carl Hanser, 1955), p. 67.

31. The matter of Scheffler's titles is worthy of some investigation. Striking differences in orthography and occasional remarkable contra-

dictions between title and content make one wonder whether the titles are actually contemporanous with the verses.

32. Cf. Czepko's less radical version of a similar idea:

> *Wir sind auch etwas.*
> Der Welt liegt viel an mir, lebt ich nicht diesen Blick
> (Ich bin ein Theil davon) das gantze gieng in Stück (II, 54).
> *We Are Also Something.*
> I mean a lot to the world; if I did not live this moment
> (I am a part of it), the whole thing would go to pieces.

33. See, for example, *Eine Deutsche Theologie,* Ch. III.

34. For examples of how Scheffler does this, see Spörri, pp. 23–24.

35. Held, III, 219.

36. Milton, *Paradise Lost,* I, 64.

37. This connection is not a critic's reconstruction. Scheffler had already used this word play in another couplet (II, 4) and explained it specifically in a note (Held, III, 219).

38. For several examples, see Neuwinger, pp. 113–14.

39. This verse is quoted from the first edition of 1657. In the second edition the second line reads: "Beym Teuffel in der Höll da ist ein ewges leid" ("With the Devil in Hell there is eternal suffering"). Whether this is an intended revision of Scheffler's or simply an error is uncertain.

40. James, *Varieties of Religious Experience,* p. 407.

41. *Eine Deutsche Theologie,* p. 180.

42. Held, III, 220.

43. Cf. T. S. Eliot's "Waste Land," where the concept of death eventually becomes a symbol for the renewal of life, or Goethe's phrase, *Stirb und werde* ("Die and become").

44. Ellinger, *Lebensbild,* p. 114.

45. Held, III, 219.

46. *Deutsche Dichtung von der Renaissance bis zum Ausgang des Barock* (2nd ed.; Darmstadt: Wissenschaftliche Buchgesellschaft, 1957), p. 227.

47. Baumgardt, *Great Western Mystics,* p. 64.

48. *Johannis Angeli Silesii Cherubinischer Wanders-Mann* (Frankfurt am Main: J. D. Zunner, 1701).

49. See Held, I, 84; Neuwinger, pp. 213–16; Ellinger, *Lebensbild,* pp. 123–25.

50. The passages are collected in Held, I, 171–72, n. 110.

51. For a bibliography of nineteenth-century editions and excerpts, see *Der cherubinische Wandersmann,* ed. Charles Waldemar, Gold-

manns Gelbe Taschenbücher, No. 607 (Munich: Wilhelm Goldmann, 1960), pp. 232–33.

52. Angelus Silesius, *Geistliche Sprüche aus dem Cherubinischen Wandersmann* (Berlin: Dümmler, 1820); *Angelus Silesius und Saint-Martin. Auszüge* (Berlin: Viet und Comp., 1834). A copy in the Yale University Library with the imprint 1833 and no publisher seems to have been privately printed by Varnhagen for his and his wife's friends.

53. Held published this essay separately: Friedrich Schlegel, *Anfangspunkte des christlichen Nachdenkens. Nach den Sprüchen des Cherubinischen Wandersmanns* (Munich: Hans Sachs-Verlag, 1917).

54. See Held, I, 180–81, n. 114a.

55. "Nach dem Angelus Silesius," Droste-Hülshoff, *Sämtliche Werke,* ed. Clemens Heselhaus (Munich: Carl Hanser, 1963), pp. 20–22.

56. Thomas Mann, *Doktor Faustus* (Stockholm: Bermann-Fischer, 1948), p. 211.

57. See Hildegard Aust, "Johann Scheffler—Silesius," *Stimmen der Zeit,* CLXII (1958), p. 264.

Chapter Three

1. James, *Varieties of Religious Experience,* p. 341.

2. For references to Bach's use of *Kontrafaktur,* see Paul Merker and Wolfgang Stammler, *Reallexikon der deutschen Literaturgeschichte* (2nd ed., I; Berlin: W. de Gruyter, 1958), 882–83.

3. Ellinger, *Lebensbild,* pp. 148–52; see also Held, I, 145–48.

4. All quotations from the *Holy Joy of the Soul* are taken from the original of the second edition, *Heilige Seelen-Lust/ oder Geistliche Hirten-Lieder/ Der in Jhren JESUM verliebten Psyche* (Breslau: Baumannische Erben, 1668), in the Beinecke Rare Book Library of Yale University.

5. Held, I, 303.

6. *Ibid.*

7. Joseph was choirmaster to Sebastian Rostock. See Robert Eitner, *Biographisches-Bibliographisches Quellen-Lexikon der Musiker und Musikgelehrten* (Leipzig: Breitkopf & Haertel, 1900–1904), *sub* Joseph, V, 303–4. Joseph seems to be chiefly remembered for this work.

8. Held, I, 304.

9. For a discussion of the place occupied by the *Holy Joy of the Soul* in the history of the German lyric see Günther Müller, *Geschichte des deutschen Liedes* (Munich: Drei Masken-Verlag, 1925), pp. 150–53.

10. Metrical purists may object to calling a line dactylic which contains only one dactylic foot preceded by an upbeat and followed by a trochee (xxxxx). Without wishing to argue the point, I will say only

that reading the poem aloud brings the dactylic foot of the inner lines into such prominence and makes the trochee so obviously an apocopated reiteration of the rhythm of the preceding foot, that to speak of a dactylic sound in contrast to the preceding iambs seems completely justified.

11. Opitz, *Buch von der Deutschen Poeterey*, p. 36.

12. *Ibid.*, p. 21.

13. Scheffler's version seems dependent on Luther, who translates the Hebrew *ta'arog* ("longs for, craves") as *schreit nach* ("cries for"). This is another example of the pervasiveness of Luther's translation even among Catholics, despite all polemicizing against it; something which Luther in his own time had occasion to point out with glee.

Chapter Four

1. Held, I, 99.

2. Ellinger, *Lebensbild*, p. 198.

3. Held, I, 319.

4. *Ibid.*

5. Held, I, 320.

6. *Ibid.*

7. Details in Held, I, 196–212.

8. See Held, I, 195, n. 124.

9. Held, I, 108.

10. All verses are quoted from Held's edition. This is unfortunately a normalized text; the original is rare and was not available to me.

11. Ellinger, *Lebensbild*, p. 203.

Chapter Five

1. W. Schrader, *Angelus Silesius und seine Mystik* (Halle: Anton, 1853). August Kahlert, in *Angelus Silesius, eine literar-historische Untersuchung* (Breslau: Gosohorsky, 1853), quickly refuted this without difficulty.

2. The most comprehensive, though biased and uncritical, accounts of the *Ecclesiologia* are to be found in Edith Eilert, *Angelus Silesius als Streittheologe seiner Zeit* (Dresden: M. Dilbert & Co., 1936); and M. Hilde Godeker, *Angelus Silesius' Personality through His Ecclesiologia* (Washington, D. C.: The Catholic University of America Press, 1938).

3. All references are to the Yale copy of the *Ecclesiologia*. See above, Chapter 1, n. 45.

4. See the amusing reprint by Schertzer of one of Scheffler's pamphlets supplied with marginal refutations, Held, I, 291.

5. Schertzer, *Und Scheffler redet noch so viel als nichts*, p. 46.

Notes and References

6. See Hajo Holborn, *A History of Modern Germany. The Reformation* (New York: Alfred A. Knopf, 1961), p. 212.

7. *Kurtze Erörterung der Frage/ Ob die Lutheraner in Schlesien/ der in Instrumento Pacis denen Augsburgischen Confessions-Verwandten verliehenen Religions-Freyheit/ sich getrösten können* (cols. dcclvii–dcclxxvi); *Verthätigte Erörterung der Frage/ Ob die Lutheraner in Schlesien/ der in Instrumento Pacis denen Augsburgischen Confessions-Verwandten verliehenen Religions-Freyheit/ sich getrösten können* (cols. dcclxxv–dcccxlii); *Paraenesis Controversistica* (cols. dcccxli–dccccxxx).

8. See Schertzer, *Und Scheffler redet noch so viel als nichts*, pp. 37–38.

Selected Bibliography

ORIGINAL EDITIONS

Johannis Angeli Silesii Geistreiche Sinn- und Schlußreime. Vienna: J. J. Kürner, 1657.

Heilige Seelen-Lust| Oder Geistliche Hirten-Lieder| Der in jhren JESUM verliebten Psyche, Gesungen von Johann Angelo Silesio, Und von Herren Georgio Josepho mit außbundig schönen Melodeyen geziert| Allen liebhabenden Seelen zur Ergetzlichkeit und Vermehrung jhrer heiligen Liebe zu Lob und Ehren Gottes an den Tag gegeben. Breslau: Baumannische Drukkerey [1657].

Johannis Angeli und Georgii Josephi Vierdter Theil der Geistlichen Hirten-Lieder| zu der verliebten Psyche gehörig. Bestehende in allerhand Schönen Anmutungen und neuen Melodeyen. Breslau: [Baumannische Drukkerey, 1657].

Heilige Seelen-Lust oder Geistliche Hirten-Lieder| Der in jhren JESUM verliebten Psyche| Gesungen von Johann Angelo Silesio, Und von Herren Georgio Josepho mit außbündig schönen Melodeyen geziert. Anjetzo auffs neue übersehn| und mit dem Fünfften Theil vermehrt. Allen denen die nicht singen können statt eines andächtigen Gebet-Buchs zu gebrauchen. Breslau: Baumannische Erben Druckerey, 1668.

J. A. Silesij Sinnliche Beschreibung Der Vier Letzten Dinge| Zu heilsamen Schröken und Auffmunterung aller Menschen inn Druck gegeben. Mit der himlischen Procession vermehrt. Schweidnitz: Gottfried Jonisches Drukkerey, 1675 [i.e., 1674].

Johannis Angeli Silesij Cherubinischer Wandersmann oder Geist-Reiche Sinn- und Schluß -Reime zur Göttlichen beschaulichkeit anleitende. Von dem Urheber aufs neue übersehn| und mit dem Sechsten Buch vermehrt| den Liebhabern der geheimen Theologie und beschaulichen Lebens zur Geistlichen Ergötzlichkeit zum andernmahl herauß gegeben. Glatz: Ignatius Schubarth, 1675.

Joh: Angeli Silesij Köstliche Evangelische Perle Zur Vollkommener ausschmuckung der Brautt Christi. Glatz: Ignatius Schubarth, 1676.

D. Johannis Schefflers Der H. Römischen Kirchen Pristers Ecclesiologia Oder Kirche-Be-schreibung. Bestehende in Neun und dreyssig unterschiedenen außerlesenen Tractätlein von der Catholischen Kirche und dero wahren Glauben/ wie auch von den Uncatholischen Gelachen und dero falschem Wahn/ so theils vorhin absonderlich gedrukt worden/ theils aber noch nie das Tagelicht gesehen. Mit einem allgemeinen Anzeiger/ in welchem die in denen Tractätlein behaltene allerhand schöne Materien alsbald erkennt werden können. Allen so wol Catholischen zur Stärkung im Glauben als Uncatholischen zuerleuchtung höchst nöthig; Sonderlich aber denen Pfarrherrn und Predigern zu unterweisung ihrer Kirch-Kinder und Zuehörer sehr nützlich: Denen aber die in Uncatholischen Oertern den Glauben fortpflantzen sollen/ und entweder wegen mangel der Bücher oder Beschäfftigung nicht Studiren können zu absonderlichen Nachdruk dienlich. Neiss and Glatz: Ignatius Schubarth, 1677.

MODERN EDITIONS

1. Complete Editions

Angelus Silesius. *Sämtliche poetische Werke und eine Auswahl aus seinen Streitschriften.* Ed. Georg Ellinger. Berlin: Propyläen-Verlag, [1923]. 2 vols. Still the definitive edition; text slightly normalized. The 195-page introduction is a standard source of information.

————. *Sämtliche poetische Werke.* Ed. Hans Ludwig Held. Munich: Allgemeine Verlagsanstalt, 1922, 2 vols.

————. *Sämtliche poetische Werke.* Ed. Hans Ludwig Held. 2nd ed. Munich: Allgemeine Verlagsanstalt, 1924. 2 vols.

————. *Sämtliche poetische Werke.* Ed. Hans Ludwig Held. 3rd ed. Munich: Carl Hanser Verlag, 1952. 3 vols. The third edition is an expanded and revised version of the first two and is the one most easily available to modern readers. Its advantage is that it contains a great deal of documentation and materials in 102 pages of notes and 140 pages of collateral sources.

2. Individual Works

Heilige Seelen-Lust. Ed. Georg Ellinger. Neudrucke deutscher litteraturwerke des xvi. und xvii. jahrhunderts, Nos. 177–81. Halle: Max Niemeyer, 1901. Incorporated into Ellinger's complete edition.

Cherubinischer Wandersmann. Ed. Georg Ellinger. Neudrucke deutscher litteraturwerke des xvi. und xvii. jahrhunderts, Nos. 135–38.

Selected Bibliography

Halle: Max Niemeyer, 1895. Incorporated into Ellinger's complete edition.

Cherubinischer Wandersmann. Ed. Will-Erich Peuckert. Bremen: Carl Schünemann [1956]. An excellent individual edition with an informative commentary.

Der cherubinische Wandersmann. Ed. Charles Waldemar. Munich: Wilhelm Goldmann Verlag, 1960. Goldmanns Gelbe Taschenbücher, No. 607. Contains also selections from the *Heilige Seelen-Lust.* An easily available and inexpensive edition, although in painfully small print. The normalization of the text and the bibliographical apparatus have been severely criticized.

TRANSLATIONS

Angelus Silesius. *A Selection from the Rhymes of a German Mystic.* Trans. Paul Carus. Chicago: The Open Court Publishing Company, 1909. Contains 153 verses from the *Cherubinischer Wandersmann* with the original German. The meter is maintained, but the Alexandrine form is somewhat obscured by the printing of couplets as four-line verses.

Angelus Silesius. *Selections from The Cherubinic Wanderer.* Trans. J. E. Crawford Flitch. London: George Allen & Unwin Ltd., 1932. Contains 355 verses with the German in an appendix. Many of the translations are very felicitous. The eighty-three-page introduction is one of the best essays on Scheffler available in English.

Alexandrines Translated from the "Cherubinischer Wandersmann" of Angelus Silesius 1657. North Montpelier, Vt.: The Driftwind Press, 1944. Trans. Julia Bilger. With 376 verses, the largest of the available translations. Concentrates on felicity rather than literal accuracy; a very talented performance.

Angelus Silesius. *The Cherubinic Wanderer. Selections.* Trans. Willard R. Trask. Introduction by Curt von Faber du Faur. New York: Pantheon Books, Inc., 1953. Contains 140 verses, of which 83 are taken from Book I. They are arranged in four-line verses. The brief introduction is by an outstanding expert on the German Baroque.

SECONDARY SOURCES

Althaus, Horst. *Johann Schefflers "Cherubinischer Wandersmann": Mystik und Dichtung.* Giessen: Wilhelm Schmitz, 1956. (Beiträge zur deutschen Philologie, Vol. IX.) This is one of the best and most lucid of recent studies. Althaus identifies and defines the major issues in an exemplary way.

Aust, Hildegard. "Johannes Scheffler—Silesius." *Stimmen der Zeit,* CLXII (1958), 258–70. A general study from a modern Catholic point of view. Contains some interesting points on Scheffler's influence.

Baruzi, Jean. *Création religieuse et pensée contemplative. I. La mystique paulienne et les données autobiographiques des épîtres. II. Angelus Silesius.* Paris: Aubier, 1951. A sophisticated treatment from the point of view of the nature of mystical thinking.

Eilert, Edith. *Angelus Silesius als Streittheologe seiner Zeit.* Dresden: M. Dilkert & Co., 1936. A study of the *Ecclesiologia* which, despite its strong Catholic bias, is interesting because it treats every pamphlet and makes useful observations upon Scheffler's opposition to political solutions.

Ellinger, Georg. "Angelus Silesius." *Westermanns Monatshefte,* CXXXVII (1924/25), 288–92. A brief popular introduction.

———. *Angelus Silesius. Ein Lebensbild.* Breslau: Wilh. Gottl. Korn, 1927. An expanded version of the introduction to Ellinger's complete edition with more extensive documentation.

Gies, M. Hildburgis. *Eine lateinische Quelle zum "Cherubinischen Wandersmann" des Angelus Silesius. Untersuchung der Beziehungen zwischen der mystischen Dichtung Schefflers und der "Clavis pro theologia mystica" des Maximilian Sandaeus.* Breslau: Müller & Seiffert, 1929. Breslauer Studien zur historischen Theologie, Vol. XII. The most important single study of Scheffler's sources, establishing this compendium as a major inspiration for his mystical expressions.

Godeker, M. Hilde. *Angelus Silesius' Personality Through His Ecclesiologia.* Washington, D. C.: The Catholic University of America Press, 1938. One of two studies of the *Ecclesiologia.* Unfortunately, it does not deal with Scheffler's personality but represents an uncritical acceptance of his arguments.

Hesse, Hermann. "Angelus Silesius." In: *Betrachtungen.* Berlin: S. Fischer, 1928, pp. 231–35. A characterization of Scheffler by an outstanding writer. Not included in Hesse's later editions.

Kahlert, August. *Angelus Silesius, eine literar-historische Untersuchung.* Breslau: Gosohorsky, 1853. The beginning of scholarly studies on Scheffler. Much of the subsequent scholarship is based on this work.

Karrer, Otto. "Angelus Silesius." *Hochland,* XXVIII, pt. 2 (1931), 297–344. An argument that Scheffler's mysticism can only be understood in a Catholic context.

Kern, Franz. *Johann Scheffler's Cherubinischer Wandersmann. Eine literarhistorische Untersuchung.* Leipzig: S. Hirzel, 1866. Despite its age, a study not without substantial and interesting insights into the character of the work.

König, Paula. "Die mystische Lehre des Angelus Silesius in religions-philosophischer und psychologischer Deutung." Diss. Munich, 1942. An unpublished dissertation which examines the content of Scheffler's doctrine in isolation from the poetic work.

Langosch, K. "Die 'Heilige Seelenlust' des Angelus Silesius und die mittellateinische Hymnik." *Zeitschrift für deutsches Altertum und Literatur,* CXVII (1930), 155–68. The only individual study of the *Heilige Seelen-Lust.* It supplements the sources noted by Ellinger and Held.

Linde, Fritz. "Das Gegensätzliche in Johann Schefflers Lebensgefühl." Diss. Leipzig, 1924. A formal study which provided part of the basis for Benno von Wiese's article (see below).

Lindemann, Wilhelm. *Angelus Silesius, Bild eines Konvertiten, Dichters und Streittheologen aus dem 17. Jahrhundert.* Freiburg im Breisgau: Herder, 1876. A moderate Catholic view of Scheffler which was sharply attacked by the more extreme Catholic scholars, Seltmann and Richstätter.

Neuwinger, Rudolf. *Johann Schefflers "Cherubinischer Wandersmann" und die deutsche Mystik.* Blecherode am Harz: Carl Nieft, 1937. An attempt to place Scheffler in a putative pantheistic tradition of "German mysticism." The latter concept has unfortunate connections to the Nazi version of "German religion," but Neuwinger's book, though its judgments must be regarded with some caution, is free of hateful excesses, philologically sound, and rich in enlightening comparisons.

Orcibal, Jean. "Les sources étrangères du 'Cherubinischer Wandersmann' (1657) d'après la bibliothèque d'Angelus Silesius." *Revue de littérature comparée,* XVIII (1938), 494–506. A fine compact study of probable influences from books Scheffler is known to have owned.

Palmer, Frederick. "Angelus Silesius. A Seventeenth-Century Mystic." *Harvard Theological Review,* XI (1918), 171–202. A comprehensive general introduction for the English-speaking reader.

Petersen, Grethe Wagner. "Zur Datierung und Deutung von Angelus Silesius: 'Cherubinischer Wandersmann,'" *Orbis Litterarum,* III (1945), 139–87. A new attempt at dating; particularly interesting with respect to connections found between Book III and the festivals of the saints.

Plard, Henri. *Pèlerin chérubinique.* Paris: Aubier, 1946. This French translation of the *Cherubinischer Wandersmann* contains an excellent introduction and the most comprehensive bibliography of secondary sources to be found anywhere.

Richstätter, Karl, S. J. "Angelus Silesius, Mystiker und Konvertit." *Stimmen der Zeit*, CXI (1926), 361–81. This and the following two articles support Seltmann's view of Scheffler's Catholic orthodoxy. Richstätter has the advantage of a more thorough knowledge of Neo-Catholic mysticism than Ellinger and Held.

————. "Angelus Silesius und sein jüngstes Lebensbild." *Zeitschrift für Askese und Mystik*, III (1927), 77–85. A critique of Ellinger's biography (see above).

————. "Barocke Mystik des Angelus Silesius." *Stimmen der Zeit*, CXXI (1931), 326–40.

Riemschneider, Ursula. "Die unio mystica in der Dichtung Daniel von Czepkos und Johann Schefflers." Diss. Strassburg, 1942. This comparison of Czepko and Scheffler provided materials for Wentzlaff-Eggebert's important study (see below).

Schäfer, Renate. *Die Negation als Ausdrucksform mit besonderer Berücksichtigung der Sprache des Angelus Silesius.* Diss. Bonn, 1959. One of the few studies of Scheffler which make use of modern critical techniques in an effort to define a significant formal element.

Schrader, W. *Angelus Silesius und seine Mystik.* Halle: Anton, 1853. A study which has chiefly curiosity value because the author attempted to prove that Angelus Silesius and Johann Scheffler were not the same person.

Schuster, Gustav. "Angelus Silesius. Ein historisch-kritischer Versuch." *Zeitschrift für die historische Theologie*, XXVII (1857), 427–58. An early attempt to identify Scheffler's sources in the tradition.

Seltmann, Carl. *Angelus Silesius und seine Mystik.* Breslau: G. P. Aderholz, 1896. The chief witness in the Catholic case for Scheffler. Seltmann's argument, though learned, is weakened by his rigid and dogmatic extremism and *a priori* assumptions.

Seyppel, Joachim H. "Freedom and the Mystical Union in *Der cherubinische Wandersmann*." *Germanic Review*, XXXII (1957), 93–112. A study of the problem of will in Scheffler's mysticism.

Spörri, Elisabeth. *Der cherubinische Wandersmann als Kunstwerk.* Horgen: Fritz Frei, 1947. This study, originally a dissertation for Emil Staiger at the University of Zurich, is the most thorough formal examination of Scheffler's art and is indispensable for further scholarship.

Tarracó, Jaime. "Angelus Silesius und die spanische Mystik. Die Wirkung der spanischen Mystik auf den Cherubinischen Wanders-

mann." In: *Gesammelte Aufsätze zur Kulturgeschichte Spaniens*
(Görres-Gesellschaft, Spanische Forschungen, Reihe I), XV, 1–
150. Münster: Aschendorffsche Verlags-Buchhandlung, 1960. A
study of the important influence of Neo-Catholic Spanish mysticism on Scheffler.

Viëtor, Karl. "Johann Scheffler." In: *Geist und Form. Aufsätze zur
deutschen Literaturgeschichte*. Berne: A. Francke, 1952, pp. 53–
64. An impressionistic essay by an able scholar.

Wentzlaff-Eggebert, Friedrich-Wilhelm. *Deutsche Mystik zwischen
Mittelalter und Neuzeit*. Berlin: Walter de Gruyter & Co., 1944.
Published in the darkest days of the war, yet lacking a single
phrase conciliatory to the Nazi abomination, this work is very useful for placing Scheffler in the perspective of his tradition and particularly in working out the connection to Daniel von Czepko and
other contemporaries.

Wiese, Benno von. "Die Antithetik in den Alexandrinern des Angelus
Silesius." *Euphorion*, XXIX (1928), 503–22. One of the earliest
studies applying modern critical techniques to Scheffler's form.
Von Wiese compares related patterns in a most useful way.

Index